Contents

▷▷▷▷▷▷▷▷▷▷▷▷▷▷▷▷

◀ **Use What You Know** ▶

Shapes and Fractions

Measurement

Place Value • Numbers to 1,000

Adding and Subtracting 3-Digit Numbers

Exploring Multiplication and Division

Joining Groups

Use the pictures.
Write the sums.

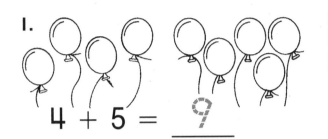

1. $4 + 5 = \underline{9}$

2. $7 + 1 = \underline{\hspace{1cm}}$

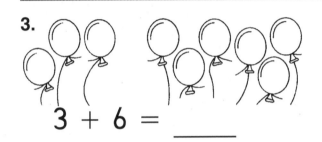

3. $3 + 6 = \underline{\hspace{1cm}}$

4. $2 + 6 = \underline{\hspace{1cm}}$

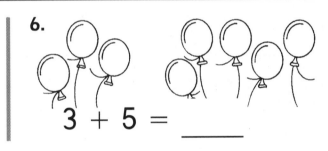

5. $5 + 2 = \underline{\hspace{1cm}}$

6. $3 + 5 = \underline{\hspace{1cm}}$

7. $4 + 2 = \underline{\hspace{1cm}}$

8. $1 + 5 = \underline{\hspace{1cm}}$

Number Sense

9. Which pair has the greatest sum?
   Ring the pair.

$9 + 3$ $9 + 2$ $9 + 5$ $9 + 1$

Order and Zero Properties

Write the sums.

1.
$$\begin{array}{r} 0 \\ +8 \\ \hline 8 \end{array}$$
$$\begin{array}{r} 8 \\ +0 \\ \hline \end{array}$$
$$\begin{array}{r} 4 \\ +6 \\ \hline \end{array}$$
$$\begin{array}{r} 6 \\ +4 \\ \hline \end{array}$$
$$\begin{array}{r} 9 \\ +1 \\ \hline \end{array}$$
$$\begin{array}{r} 1 \\ +9 \\ \hline \end{array}$$

2.
$$\begin{array}{r} 5 \\ +3 \\ \hline \end{array}$$
$$\begin{array}{r} 3 \\ +7 \\ \hline \end{array}$$
$$\begin{array}{r} 7 \\ +6 \\ \hline \end{array}$$
$$\begin{array}{r} 0 \\ +5 \\ \hline \end{array}$$
$$\begin{array}{r} 2 \\ +6 \\ \hline \end{array}$$
$$\begin{array}{r} 8 \\ +2 \\ \hline \end{array}$$

3.
$$\begin{array}{r} 6 \\ +0 \\ \hline \end{array}$$
$$\begin{array}{r} 9 \\ +3 \\ \hline \end{array}$$
$$\begin{array}{r} 3 \\ +6 \\ \hline \end{array}$$
$$\begin{array}{r} 0 \\ +4 \\ \hline \end{array}$$
$$\begin{array}{r} 5 \\ +4 \\ \hline \end{array}$$
$$\begin{array}{r} 9 \\ +0 \\ \hline \end{array}$$

Visual Thinking

Ring the train that has the fewest cubes.

4.

5.

Use with text pages 5–6.

Adding on a Number Line

Draw lines to match.

1.

$1 + 6 = 7$

2.

$3 + 6 = 9$

3.

$0 + 3 = 3$

4.

$5 + 4 = 9$

5.

$8 + 2 = 10$

6.

$6 + 3 = 9$

Story Corner

7. Tell a story.
   Write an addition sentence.

_____ + _____ = _____

_____ children

Counting On

Count on to add.

1.
$$\begin{array}{r} 8 \\ +2 \\ \hline 10 \end{array}$$
$$\begin{array}{r} 6 \\ +1 \\ \hline \end{array}$$
$$\begin{array}{r} 5 \\ +2 \\ \hline \end{array}$$
$$\begin{array}{r} 8 \\ +3 \\ \hline \end{array}$$
$$\begin{array}{r} 7 \\ +1 \\ \hline \end{array}$$
$$\begin{array}{r} 9 \\ +2 \\ \hline \end{array}$$

2.
$$\begin{array}{r} 9 \\ +1 \\ \hline \end{array}$$
$$\begin{array}{r} 5 \\ +3 \\ \hline \end{array}$$
$$\begin{array}{r} 6 \\ +2 \\ \hline \end{array}$$
$$\begin{array}{r} 4 \\ +2 \\ \hline \end{array}$$
$$\begin{array}{r} 7 \\ +3 \\ \hline \end{array}$$
$$\begin{array}{r} 8 \\ +1 \\ \hline \end{array}$$

3.
$$\begin{array}{r} 3 \\ +1 \\ \hline \end{array}$$
$$\begin{array}{r} 3 \\ +2 \\ \hline \end{array}$$
$$\begin{array}{r} 2 \\ +1 \\ \hline \end{array}$$
$$\begin{array}{r} 9 \\ +3 \\ \hline \end{array}$$
$$\begin{array}{r} 8 \\ +2 \\ \hline \end{array}$$
$$\begin{array}{r} 4 \\ +1 \\ \hline \end{array}$$

4.
$$\begin{array}{r} 3 \\ +2 \\ \hline \end{array}$$
$$\begin{array}{r} 5 \\ +1 \\ \hline \end{array}$$
$$\begin{array}{r} 4 \\ +3 \\ \hline \end{array}$$
$$\begin{array}{r} 3 \\ +3 \\ \hline \end{array}$$
$$\begin{array}{r} 7 \\ +2 \\ \hline \end{array}$$
$$\begin{array}{r} 6 \\ +3 \\ \hline \end{array}$$

Reasoning

Write the missing number.

5.

6.

Use with text pages 9–10.

More Counting On

Ring the greater number.
Then count on to add.

1.
$$\begin{array}{r} 2 \\ +5 \\ \hline 7 \end{array}$$
$$\begin{array}{r} 8 \\ +1 \\ \hline \end{array}$$
$$\begin{array}{r} 5 \\ +3 \\ \hline \end{array}$$
$$\begin{array}{r} 1 \\ +6 \\ \hline \end{array}$$
$$\begin{array}{r} 7 \\ +2 \\ \hline \end{array}$$
$$\begin{array}{r} 3 \\ +7 \\ \hline \end{array}$$

2.
$$\begin{array}{r} 1 \\ +4 \\ \hline \end{array}$$
$$\begin{array}{r} 3 \\ +4 \\ \hline \end{array}$$
$$\begin{array}{r} 4 \\ +2 \\ \hline \end{array}$$
$$\begin{array}{r} 9 \\ +1 \\ \hline \end{array}$$
$$\begin{array}{r} 2 \\ +6 \\ \hline \end{array}$$
$$\begin{array}{r} 2 \\ +8 \\ \hline \end{array}$$

3.
$$\begin{array}{r} 2 \\ +9 \\ \hline \end{array}$$
$$\begin{array}{r} 7 \\ +1 \\ \hline \end{array}$$
$$\begin{array}{r} 8 \\ +3 \\ \hline \end{array}$$
$$\begin{array}{r} 6 \\ +3 \\ \hline \end{array}$$
$$\begin{array}{r} 3 \\ +5 \\ \hline \end{array}$$
$$\begin{array}{r} 2 \\ +4 \\ \hline \end{array}$$

4.
$$\begin{array}{r} 9 \\ +3 \\ \hline \end{array}$$
$$\begin{array}{r} 7 \\ +3 \\ \hline \end{array}$$
$$\begin{array}{r} 3 \\ +6 \\ \hline \end{array}$$
$$\begin{array}{r} 2 \\ +8 \\ \hline \end{array}$$
$$\begin{array}{r} 1 \\ +5 \\ \hline \end{array}$$
$$\begin{array}{r} 3 \\ +1 \\ \hline \end{array}$$

Reasoning

Write the missing number.

5.

_____

6.

_____

Problem-Solving Strategy
Make a Model

Use the problem-solving
steps to solve each problem.
Use counters. Then write
the number sentence.

| Understand |
| Plan |
| Solve |
| Look Back |

1. Sal saw 3 shows at the
   fair. Then he saw 2
   more. How many shows
   did he see?

   $\underline{3} \; (+) \; \underline{2} = \underline{5}$

   _____ shows

2. Donna won 5 prizes.
   Then she won 2 more.
   How many prizes did
   she win?

   ____ ◯ ____ = ____

   _____ prizes

3. Donna had 6 tickets for
   rides. Hector had 3
   tickets. How many
   tickets did they have?

   ____ ◯ ____ = ____

   _____ tickets

4. Hector saw 4 mirrors
   in the Fun House.
   Then he saw 3 more.
   How many did he see?

   ____ ◯ ____ = ____

   _____ mirrors

Story Corner

5. Tell a story.
   Write an addition sentence.

   ____ ◯ ____ = ____

   _____ children

Joining and Separating Groups

Use counters.
Write the number sentences.

1.

$$\underline{1} \; \bigoplus \; \underline{4} = \underline{5}$$

2.

$$\underline{5} \; \bigodot \; \underline{4} = \underline{1}$$

3.

$$\underline{} \; \bigcirc \; \underline{} = \underline{}$$

4.

$$\underline{} \; \bigcirc \; \underline{} = \underline{}$$

5.

$$\underline{} \; \bigcirc \; \underline{} = \underline{}$$

6.

$$\underline{} \; \bigcirc \; \underline{} = \underline{}$$

7.

$$\underline{} \; \bigcirc \; \underline{} = \underline{}$$

8.

$$\underline{} \; \bigcirc \; \underline{} = \underline{}$$

Number Sense

9. Which number sentence has the greatest
answer? Ring it.

$$10 - 2 = ? \quad 10 - 4 = ? \quad 10 + 2 = ? \quad 10 + 4 = ?$$

Zeros in Subtraction

Subtract.

1. $3 - 3 =$ __0__

$5 - 0 =$ ____

$4 - 4 =$ ____

2. $6 - 0 =$ ____

$7 - 7 =$ ____

$9 - 9 =$ ____

3. $4 - 0 =$ ____

$6 - 6 =$ ____

$8 - 0 =$ ____

4. $8 - 8 =$ ____

$7 - 0 =$ ____

$1 - 0 =$ ____

5.
$$\begin{array}{r} 2 \\ -2 \\ \hline \end{array} \qquad \begin{array}{r} 3 \\ -0 \\ \hline \end{array} \qquad \begin{array}{r} 1 \\ -1 \\ \hline \end{array} \qquad \begin{array}{r} 9 \\ -0 \\ \hline \end{array} \qquad \begin{array}{r} 5 \\ -5 \\ \hline \end{array}$$

Story Corner

6. Look at the picture.
   Make up a story problem.
   Ask a friend to solve it.

____ ◯ ____ = ____

Use with text pages 19–20.

Subtracting on a Number Line

● Write the number sentence
that the number line shows.

I.

5 (＋) 3 = 8

2.

◯

_____ _____ = _____

3.

◯

_____ _____ = _____

4.

◯

_____ _____ = _____

Visual Thinking

5. Ring the number line that shows subtraction.

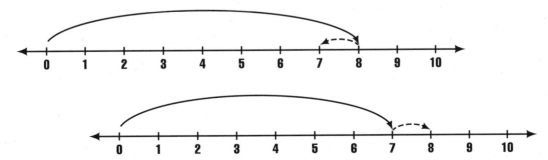

Counting Back

Subtract.

1.
$$\begin{array}{r} 6 \\ -2 \\ \hline 4 \end{array}$$
6, 5, 4
$$\begin{array}{r} 9 \\ -2 \\ \hline \end{array}$$
$$\begin{array}{r} 5 \\ -1 \\ \hline \end{array}$$
$$\begin{array}{r} 3 \\ -1 \\ \hline \end{array}$$
$$\begin{array}{r} 10 \\ -2 \\ \hline \end{array}$$

2.
$$\begin{array}{r} 7 \\ -1 \\ \hline \end{array}$$
$$\begin{array}{r} 4 \\ -2 \\ \hline \end{array}$$
$$\begin{array}{r} 8 \\ -2 \\ \hline \end{array}$$
$$\begin{array}{r} 2 \\ -1 \\ \hline \end{array}$$
$$\begin{array}{r} 10 \\ -1 \\ \hline \end{array}$$
$$\begin{array}{r} 5 \\ -2 \\ \hline \end{array}$$

3.
$$\begin{array}{r} 8 \\ -1 \\ \hline \end{array}$$
$$\begin{array}{r} 7 \\ -2 \\ \hline \end{array}$$
$$\begin{array}{r} 9 \\ -1 \\ \hline \end{array}$$
$$\begin{array}{r} 3 \\ -2 \\ \hline \end{array}$$
$$\begin{array}{r} 6 \\ -1 \\ \hline \end{array}$$
$$\begin{array}{r} 4 \\ -1 \\ \hline \end{array}$$

Problem Solving

Write a number sentence to solve.

4. Lou wins 4 bears.
He gives 2 away.
How many bears does
he have left?

____ ◯ ____ = ____

____ bears

5. Sara sees 6 elves.
Then I runs away.
How many elves
are left?

____ ◯ ____ = ____

____ elves

More Counting Back

Count back to subtract.

1. Say 10. (9, 8)

$10 - 2 =$ __8__

2. Say 8. (7, 6, 5)

$8 - 3 =$ ____

3. Say 9. (8, 7, 6)

$9 - 3 =$ ____

4. Say 8. (7)

$8 - 1 =$ ____

5.
9	9	10	8	9	10
-2	-1	-3	-2	-3	-1

Number Sense
Use a calculator.
Write the answer.

6. [ON/C] [6] $-$ [2] $-$ [2] $-$ [2] $=$ ____

7. [ON/C] [8] $-$ [2] $-$ [2] $-$ [2] $-$ [2] $=$ ____

Counting Up

Ring the number that is less.
Then count up to find the difference.

1.
$$\begin{array}{r} 4 \\ -2 \\ \hline 2 \end{array}$$
$$\begin{array}{r} 3 \\ -2 \\ \hline \end{array}$$
$$\begin{array}{r} 10 \\ -9 \\ \hline \end{array}$$
$$\begin{array}{r} 5 \\ -2 \\ \hline \end{array}$$
$$\begin{array}{r} 7 \\ -5 \\ \hline \end{array}$$
$$\begin{array}{r} 4 \\ -3 \\ \hline \end{array}$$

2.
$$\begin{array}{r} 9 \\ -6 \\ \hline \end{array}$$
$$\begin{array}{r} 8 \\ -7 \\ \hline \end{array}$$
$$\begin{array}{r} 6 \\ -4 \\ \hline \end{array}$$
$$\begin{array}{r} 7 \\ -4 \\ \hline \end{array}$$
$$\begin{array}{r} 5 \\ -4 \\ \hline \end{array}$$
$$\begin{array}{r} 8 \\ -5 \\ \hline \end{array}$$

3.
$$\begin{array}{r} 5 \\ -3 \\ \hline \end{array}$$
$$\begin{array}{r} 8 \\ -6 \\ \hline \end{array}$$
$$\begin{array}{r} 9 \\ -8 \\ \hline \end{array}$$
$$\begin{array}{r} 6 \\ -5 \\ \hline \end{array}$$
$$\begin{array}{r} 10 \\ -7 \\ \hline \end{array}$$
$$\begin{array}{r} 9 \\ -7 \\ \hline \end{array}$$

4.
$$\begin{array}{r} 6 \\ -3 \\ \hline \end{array}$$
$$\begin{array}{r} 7 \\ -6 \\ \hline \end{array}$$
$$\begin{array}{r} 10 \\ -8 \\ \hline \end{array}$$
$$\begin{array}{r} 4 \\ -2 \\ \hline \end{array}$$
$$\begin{array}{r} 5 \\ -3 \\ \hline \end{array}$$
$$\begin{array}{r} 9 \\ -6 \\ \hline \end{array}$$

Reasoning

5. Solve.
   Dan has 10 cards.
   Dan has 1 more card than Becky.
   Becky has 1 more card than Ted.

   How many cards does Ted have? _____ cards

Fact Families

Write the fact families.

I.

  _____ ⊕ _____ ⊙ _____

7 ⊕ 3 ⊙ 10

_____ ○ _____ ○ _____

_____ ○ _____ ○ _____

_____ ○ _____ ○ _____

2.

_____ ○ _____ ○ _____

_____ ○ _____ ○ _____

_____ ○ _____ ○ _____

_____ ○ _____ ○ _____

3.

_____ ○ _____ ○ _____

_____ ○ _____ ○ _____

_____ ○ _____ ○ _____

_____ ○ _____ ○ _____

4.

_____ ○ _____ ○ _____

_____ ○ _____ ○ _____

_____ ○ _____ ○ _____

_____ ○ _____ ○ _____

Number Sense

5. Look at the cube train. How
   many facts are in this family? _____

Problem-Solving Strategy
Write a Number Sentence

Write a number sentence to solve.

1. Helen had 9 pennies.
   She gave away 2 of them.
   How many did she have left?

   $\underline{9}\ \bigodot\ \underline{2}\ =\ \underline{7}$

   $\underline{7}$ pennies

---

2. There are 4 roses.
   There are 6 tulips.
   How many flowers are there?

   _____ $\bigcirc$ _____ = _____

   _____ flowers

---

3. Lin buys 10 pears.
   She eats 4 of them.
   How many are left?

   _____ $\bigcirc$ _____ = _____

   _____ pears

Story Corner

4. Tell a story.
   Write a number sentence.

   _____ $\bigcirc$ _____ = _____

   _____ tickets

Doubles

Use counters.
Write the sums.

$$\begin{array}{r} 3 \\ +3 \\ \hline 6 \end{array}$$

$$\begin{array}{r} 6 \\ +6 \\ \hline 12 \end{array}$$

1.
$$\begin{array}{r} 1 \\ +1 \\ \hline 2 \end{array}\quad \begin{array}{r} 7 \\ +7 \\ \hline \end{array}\quad \begin{array}{r} 2 \\ +2 \\ \hline \end{array}\quad \begin{array}{r} 8 \\ +8 \\ \hline \end{array}\quad \begin{array}{r} 4 \\ +4 \\ \hline \end{array}\quad \begin{array}{r} 5 \\ +5 \\ \hline \end{array}$$

2.
$$\begin{array}{r} 0 \\ +0 \\ \hline \end{array}\quad \begin{array}{r} 3 \\ +3 \\ \hline \end{array}\quad \begin{array}{r} 6 \\ +6 \\ \hline \end{array}\quad \begin{array}{r} 1 \\ +1 \\ \hline \end{array}\quad \begin{array}{r} 8 \\ +8 \\ \hline \end{array}\quad \begin{array}{r} 7 \\ +7 \\ \hline \end{array}$$

Write the sums. Then ring doubles.

3.
$$\begin{array}{r} 3 \\ +2 \\ \hline \end{array}\quad \begin{array}{r} 6 \\ +4 \\ \hline \end{array}\quad \begin{array}{r} 4 \\ +4 \\ \hline \end{array}\quad \begin{array}{r} 7 \\ +2 \\ \hline \end{array}\quad \begin{array}{r} 3 \\ +3 \\ \hline \end{array}\quad \begin{array}{r} 5 \\ +5 \\ \hline \end{array}$$

Problem Solving

4. Tony found 2 shells. David found the same number. How many shells did the boys find in all?

_____ shells

5. Rosa saw 3 crabs in the sand. She saw the same number in the water. How many crabs did she see?

_____ crabs

Doubles Plus One

Ring the numbers in each pair that have the greater sum. Then write the sums.

1.
```
   4    (4)        3    3          6    5
 + 4   + 5       + 4  + 3        + 5  + 5
   8    9
```

2.
```
   6    6          2    2          8    9
 + 7   + 6       + 2  + 3        + 8  + 8
```

Add.

Ring sums of doubles ▐ blue ▷ .

Ring sums of doubles plus one ▐ yellow ▷ .

3.
```
   3        3        2        8        7        4
 + 4      + 3      + 2      + 7      + 6      + 4
   7
```

Visual Thinking

4. Ring the pictures that show doubles plus one.

Use with text pages 43–44.

Adding 9

Add.

1.

$\begin{array}{r} 9 \\ +5 \\ \hline 14 \end{array}$

$\begin{array}{r} 10 \\ +4 \\ \hline \end{array}$

2.

$\begin{array}{r} 9 \\ +3 \\ \hline \end{array}$

$\begin{array}{r} 10 \\ +2 \\ \hline \end{array}$

3.

$\begin{array}{r} 9 \\ +8 \\ \hline \end{array}$

$\begin{array}{r} 10 \\ +7 \\ \hline \end{array}$

4. $\begin{array}{r} 9 \\ +4 \\ \hline \end{array}$ (Think. 10 + 3) $\begin{array}{r} 9 \\ +6 \\ \hline \end{array}$ $\begin{array}{r} 9 \\ +7 \\ \hline \end{array}$ $\begin{array}{r} 8 \\ +9 \\ \hline \end{array}$ $\begin{array}{r} 3 \\ +9 \\ \hline \end{array}$

Number Sense

Ring the two that name the same number.

5. 9 + 2   10 + 3   10 + 1

6. 10 + 3   9 + 4   10 + 4

Make a 10

Use a 10-frame and counters.
Find the sums.

1.
$$\begin{array}{r} 7 \\ +6 \\ \hline 13 \end{array}$$
$$\begin{array}{r} 9 \\ +3 \\ \hline \end{array}$$
$$\begin{array}{r} 5 \\ +7 \\ \hline \end{array}$$
$$\begin{array}{r} 4 \\ +9 \\ \hline \end{array}$$
$$\begin{array}{r} 9 \\ +6 \\ \hline \end{array}$$
$$\begin{array}{r} 8 \\ +5 \\ \hline \end{array}$$

2.
$$\begin{array}{r} 2 \\ +9 \\ \hline \end{array}$$
$$\begin{array}{r} 8 \\ +6 \\ \hline \end{array}$$
$$\begin{array}{r} 9 \\ +5 \\ \hline \end{array}$$
$$\begin{array}{r} 6 \\ +9 \\ \hline \end{array}$$
$$\begin{array}{r} 4 \\ +7 \\ \hline \end{array}$$
$$\begin{array}{r} 9 \\ +4 \\ \hline \end{array}$$

3.
$$\begin{array}{r} 3 \\ +8 \\ \hline \end{array}$$
$$\begin{array}{r} 8 \\ +4 \\ \hline \end{array}$$
$$\begin{array}{r} 7 \\ +5 \\ \hline \end{array}$$
$$\begin{array}{r} 9 \\ +7 \\ \hline \end{array}$$
$$\begin{array}{r} 6 \\ +8 \\ \hline \end{array}$$
$$\begin{array}{r} 5 \\ +9 \\ \hline \end{array}$$

Problem Solving

Write a number sentence to solve.

4. Miko saw 7 seals. Soon 5 of them swam away. How many seals were left?

_____ ⃝ _____ = _____

_____ seals

5. Alice saw 6 baby seals and 7 mother seals. How many seals did she see?

_____ ⃝ _____ = _____

_____ seals

HRJ material copyrighted under notice appearing earlier in this work.

Use with text pages 47–48.

Adding More Than Two Addends

Sometimes, looking for a 10 or a double
makes adding easy.
Add.

1.
$\begin{array}{r} 2 \\ 2 \end{array}\}4$ $\begin{array}{r} 2 \\ 6 \\ +4 \end{array}\}10$ $\begin{array}{r} 5 \\ 3 \\ +3 \end{array}\}6$ $\begin{array}{r} 4 \\ 4 \\ +5 \end{array}\}8$ $\begin{array}{r} 8 \\ 2 \\ 1 \\ +3 \end{array}\}10$

$\begin{array}{r} +7 \\ \hline \end{array}$

2.
$\begin{array}{r} 7 \\ 5 \\ +5 \\ \hline \end{array}$ $\begin{array}{r} 8 \\ 2 \\ +7 \\ \hline \end{array}$ $\begin{array}{r} 1 \\ 4 \\ 6 \\ +3 \\ \hline \end{array}$ $\begin{array}{r} 1 \\ 8 \\ 4 \\ +4 \\ \hline \end{array}$ $\begin{array}{r} 6 \\ 4 \\ 3 \\ +2 \\ \hline \end{array}$ $\begin{array}{r} 3 \\ 3 \\ 6 \\ +1 \\ \hline \end{array}$

3.
$\begin{array}{r} 6 \\ 3 \\ +7 \\ \hline \end{array}$ $\begin{array}{r} 2 \\ 1 \\ 6 \\ +6 \\ \hline \end{array}$ $\begin{array}{r} 4 \\ 5 \\ 5 \\ +2 \\ \hline \end{array}$ $\begin{array}{r} 9 \\ 0 \\ 9 \\ +1 \\ \hline \end{array}$ $\begin{array}{r} 0 \\ 8 \\ 2 \\ +8 \\ \hline \end{array}$ $\begin{array}{r} 2 \\ 2 \\ 4 \\ +6 \\ \hline \end{array}$

Reasoning

Do these in your head.
Ring the ones with a sum greater than 10.

4. $4 + 1 + 1 + 1 + 6$ 5. $2 + 1 + 1 + 2 + 1$

6. $1 + 1 + 1 + 3 + 7$ 7. $5 + 1 + 1 + 5$

8. $1 + 1 + 1 + 1 + 1 + 1 + 1 + 1$

Sums to 14

Complete the addition sentences.

1. ⬛ 14 ⬛

$5 + \underline{9} = \underline{14}$

$6 + \underline{\hphantom{00}} = \underline{\hphantom{00}}$

$7 + \underline{\hphantom{00}} = \underline{\hphantom{00}}$

$\underline{\hphantom{00}} + \underline{\hphantom{00}} = \underline{\hphantom{00}}$

2. ⬛ 13 ⬛

$4 + \underline{\hphantom{00}} = \underline{\hphantom{00}}$

$5 + \underline{\hphantom{00}} = \underline{\hphantom{00}}$

$6 + \underline{\hphantom{00}} = \underline{\hphantom{00}}$

$\underline{\hphantom{00}} + \underline{\hphantom{00}} = \underline{\hphantom{00}}$

3. ⬛ 12 ⬛

$3 + \underline{\hphantom{00}} = \underline{\hphantom{00}}$

$4 + \underline{\hphantom{00}} = \underline{\hphantom{00}}$

$5 + \underline{\hphantom{00}} = \underline{\hphantom{00}}$

$\underline{\hphantom{00}} + \underline{\hphantom{00}} = \underline{\hphantom{00}}$

4. ⬛ 11 ⬛

$2 + \underline{\hphantom{00}} = \underline{\hphantom{00}}$

$3 + \underline{\hphantom{00}} = \underline{\hphantom{00}}$

$4 + \underline{\hphantom{00}} = \underline{\hphantom{00}}$

$\underline{\hphantom{00}} + \underline{\hphantom{00}} = \underline{\hphantom{00}}$

Reasoning

5. Continue the pattern. Write a number name on each of the last two 🦞 .

Problem Solving
Choose the Operation

Read each story.
Then write the number sentence to solve.

1. There are 5 young dolphins. There are 5 older dolphins. How many dolphins are there altogether?

$$5 \; \boxed{+} \; 5 = 10$$

2. A dolphin has 8 rings. A seal has 6 rings. How many more rings does the dolphin have than the seal?

___ ◯ ___ = ___

3. There are 11 seals on a rock. Then 2 of them dive. How many are left?

___ ◯ ___ = ___

4. A seal eats 5 small fish. Then the seal eats 7 more. How many fish does the seal eat?

___ ◯ ___ = ___

Story Corner

5. Tell a story about the picture. Write a number sentence.

___ ◯ ___ = ___

Sums to 18

Add.

1. $\begin{array}{r} 8 \\ +5 \\ \hline 13 \end{array}$ $\begin{array}{r} 7 \\ +7 \\ \hline \end{array}$ $\begin{array}{r} 5 \\ +7 \\ \hline \end{array}$ $\begin{array}{r} 9 \\ +4 \\ \hline \end{array}$ $\begin{array}{r} 9 \\ +8 \\ \hline \end{array}$ $\begin{array}{r} 6 \\ +6 \\ \hline \end{array}$

2. $\begin{array}{r} 6 \\ +8 \\ \hline \end{array}$ $\begin{array}{r} 4 \\ +7 \\ \hline \end{array}$ $\begin{array}{r} 6 \\ +8 \\ \hline \end{array}$ $\begin{array}{r} 5 \\ +9 \\ \hline \end{array}$ $\begin{array}{r} 6 \\ +9 \\ \hline \end{array}$ $\begin{array}{r} 7 \\ +6 \\ \hline \end{array}$

3. $\begin{array}{r} 9 \\ +3 \\ \hline \end{array}$ $\begin{array}{r} 9 \\ +9 \\ \hline \end{array}$ $\begin{array}{r} 7 \\ +4 \\ \hline \end{array}$ $\begin{array}{r} 6 \\ +7 \\ \hline \end{array}$ $\begin{array}{r} 8 \\ +8 \\ \hline \end{array}$ $\begin{array}{r} 4 \\ +8 \\ \hline \end{array}$

4. $\begin{array}{r} 9 \\ +8 \\ \hline \end{array}$ $\begin{array}{r} 2 \\ +9 \\ \hline \end{array}$ $\begin{array}{r} 3 \\ +9 \\ \hline \end{array}$ $\begin{array}{r} 6 \\ +5 \\ \hline \end{array}$ $\begin{array}{r} 7 \\ +5 \\ \hline \end{array}$ $\begin{array}{r} 5 \\ +6 \\ \hline \end{array}$

Problem Solving

Write a number sentence. Solve.

5. There were 11 birds in
   the air. Then 8 of the
   birds landed. How many
   birds were still in the air?

   _____ ◯ _____ = _____

   _____ birds

6. There were 5 pink birds
   and 8 white birds standing
   in the water. How many
   birds were in the water?

   _____ ◯ _____ = _____

   _____ birds

Using Doubles to Subtract

Add or subtract.
Then match.

1. $6 + 6 = \underline{12}$

2. $5 + 5 = \underline{}$

3. $9 + 9 = \underline{}$

4. $2 + 2 = \underline{}$

5. $3 + 3 = \underline{}$

6. $7 + 7 = \underline{}$

7. $4 + 4 = \underline{}$

8. $8 + 8 = \underline{}$

$10 - 5 = \underline{}$

$4 - 2 = \underline{}$

$12 - 6 = \underline{6}$

$14 - 7 = \underline{}$

$6 - 3 = \underline{}$

$18 - 9 = \underline{}$

$16 - 8 = \underline{}$

$8 - 4 = \underline{}$

Problem Solving

9. Leo put 6 orange fish
and 6 black fish in the
bowl. How many fish did
Leo put in?

_____ ◯ _____ = _____

_____ fish

10. Leo had 12 fish in his
bowl. Then he took out
6 fish to put in his tank.
How many fish were left
in the bowl?

_____ ◯ _____ = _____

_____ fish

Using Other Addition Facts to Subtract

Subtract. Then color.

Color Code	
Answer	**Color**
2	black
3	purple
4	blue
5	brown
6	yellow
7	red
8	green
9	orange

Number Sense

Do these in your head. Then write
the sums and differences.

1. 9 + 4 = 13,
   so 13 − 4 = _____ .

2. 13 − 9 = 4,
   so 4 + 9 = _____ .

3. 6 + 7 = 13,
   so 13 − 7 = _____ .

4. 13 − 6 = 7,
   so 7 + 6 = _____ .

          Use with text pages 61–62.

Related Addition and Subtraction Facts

Write the differences.

1.

Subtract 3.	
12	9
10	
11	

Subtract 5.	
11	
14	
13	

Subtract 4.	
11	
13	
12	

Subtract 6.	
14	
12	
8	

2.

Subtract 8.	
16	
12	
14	

Subtract 9.	
10	
15	
18	

Subtract 7.	
13	
16	
9	

Subtract 5.	
14	
11	
13	

3.

Subtract 6.	
10	
15	
9	

Subtract 8.	
13	
11	
15	

Subtract 9.	
11	
17	
16	

Subtract 7.	
15	
14	
10	

Problem Solving

Write a number sentence to solve.

4. There were 6 snails on the rock. There were 7 snails in the sand. How many snails were there?

____ ◯ ____ = ____

_____ snails

5. Rico had 12 shells, but he gave 3 away. How many shells did he have left?

____ ◯ ____ = ____

_____ shells

Fact Families

Complete each number sentence.
Which one does not belong to
the fact family? Ring it.

1. $15 - \underline{} = 8$

$7 + 8 = \underline{}$

$7 + 7 = \underline{}$

$\underline{} - 8 = 7$

$\underline{} + 7 = 15$

2. $7 + 9 = \underline{}$

$\underline{} - 9 = 7$

$16 - \underline{} = 9$

$9 + \underline{} = 16$

$9 + 9 = \underline{}$

3. $9 + \underline{} = 17$

$8 + \underline{} = 17$

$\underline{} - 9 = 8$

$17 - 8 = \underline{}$

$16 - 8 = \underline{}$

4. $15 - 9 = \underline{}$

$14 - 8 = \underline{}$

$6 + \underline{} = 14$

$\underline{} - 6 = 8$

$8 + 6 = \underline{}$

Number Sense

5. Write the fact family for .

$\underline{} + \underline{} = \underline{}$ $\qquad$ $\underline{} - \underline{} = \underline{}$

Using Addition and Subtraction

Add or subtract.
Use your addition table if you need to.

1. $9 + 7 =$ __16__ $16 - 7 =$ ___ $7 + 9 =$ ___

2. $5 + 8 =$ ___ $13 - 8 =$ ___ $8 + 5 =$ ___

3. $6 + 5 =$ ___ $11 - 5 =$ ___ $5 + 6 =$ ___

4.
$$\begin{array}{cccccc} 7 & 18 & 4 & 9 & 11 & 14 \\ +7 & -9 & +7 & +9 & -4 & -7 \\ \hline \end{array}$$

5.
$$\begin{array}{cccccc} 15 & 12 & 8 & 7 & 13 & 4 \\ -7 & -4 & +5 & +8 & -8 & +8 \\ \hline \end{array}$$

Problem Solving

Read each story.
Then write the number sentence to solve.

6. There were 5 red pails and 5 yellow pails in the shop. How many pails were there?

____ ◯ ____ = ____

____ pails

7. There were 5 red beach balls and 6 yellow balls in the shop. How many balls were there?

____ ◯ ____ = ____

____ balls

Problem Solving
Too Much Information

Draw a line through
the sentence that is not needed.
Then write a number sentence to solve.

1. Carolyn has 12 sea plants. ~~Josh has 6 sea plants.~~ Carolyn gives Jim 5 plants. How many plants does she have left?

   12 ⊖ 5 = 7

   7

   _____ plants

2. Kara buys 2 nets for fishing. She has 8 other nets. Kara has 4 fishing poles. How many nets does Kara have?

   _____ ◯ _____ = _____

   _____ nets

3. There are 9 men fishing. There are 8 women fishing. There are 12 boats. How many people are fishing?

   _____ ◯ _____ = _____

   _____ people

4. Marta has 11 clams. Yesterday Marta found 4 crabs. Marta has 6 fish. How many more clams does she have than fish?

   _____ ◯ _____ = _____

   _____ more clams

Story Corner

5. Tell a story about the picture. Write a number sentence.

   _____ ◯ _____ = _____

Use with text pages 69–70.

Grouping Tens

Complete the table.

How many tens? How many in all?

1.		__1__ ten	__10__ stickers in all
2.		_____ tens	_____ stickers in all
3.		_____ tens	_____ stickers in all
4.		_____ tens	_____ stickers in all
5.		_____ tens	_____ stickers in all
6.		_____ tens	_____ stickers in all

Number Sense

Which is the greater number? Ring it.

7.   30   7 tens   8.   4 tens   50

Tens and Ones

Ring groups of ten.
Write how many tens and ones.
Then write how many in all.

1. 2 tens 3 ones 23

2. ___ tens ___ ones ___

3. ___ tens ___ ones ___

4. ___ tens ___ one ___

5. ___ tens ___ one ___

6. ___ tens ___ ones ___

Visual Thinking

7. Which is easier to count? Ring it. Tell why.

Use with text pages 81–82.

Tens and Ones to 50

Write the numbers.

1.

_**34**_
_____   _____   _____

Use tens and ones.
Ring the number.

2. 3 tens   2 ones   I ten   4 ones   4 ones

  32   23   4I   I4   40   4

3. 2 tens   I one   2 tens   4 ones   3 tens

  2I   I2   42   24   30   3

Number Sense
Write the mystery numbers.

4. Emily's mystery number
   has a 2 in the tens place
   and a 5 in the ones
   place.

5. Alonzo's mystery number
   has a 7 in the tens place
   and a 4 in the ones
   place.

_____   _____

Tens and Ones to 100

Write the numbers.

1.

85
_____

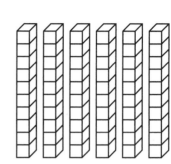

_____

2. 8 tens   7 ones   _____   **3.** 6 tens   3 ones   _____

4. 5 tens   9 ones   _____   **5.** 8 tens   6 ones   _____

Ring the number.

6. 9 tens   2 ones   6 tens   5 ones   8 ones   3 tens

  92   29   65   56   38   83

7. 7 tens   6 ones   4 ones   8 tens   9 ones   3 tens

  67   76   48   84   39   93

Visual Thinking

8.

66

Ring the better estimate.

more than 30   fewer than 30

Use with text pages 85–86.

Exchanging Dimes for Pennies

Match.

1.

2.

3.

4.

Number Sense

5. Ring the greater amount of money.

Ordering Numbers to 100

Write the month and the year.
Complete the calendar for next month.

_____

Sunday	Monday	Tuesday	Wednesday	Thursday	Friday	Saturday

Write the answers.

1. How many Fridays are in next month? _____

2. How many days are in next month? _____

Reasoning

3. Ring the numbers that end in 5 or 0.
   What skip-counting pattern do you see? Ring it.

1	2	3	4	5	6	7	8	9	10
11	12	13	14	15	16	17	18	19	20

counting by twos   counting by fives   counting by tens

Name _____

After, Before, Between

Write each hidden number.

1.

 42, 43, 44

 ___, 65, 66

 77, 78, ___

2.

 ___, 23, 24

 35, 36, ___

 82, ___, 84

3.

 12, ___, 14

 ___, 87, 88

 ___, 66, 67

4.

 ___, 60, 61

 93, ___, 95

 71, 72, ___

Reasoning

Write the missing number.
Look for a pattern.

5. 62, 64, 66, 68, 70, 72, _____

6. _____, 30, 40, 50, 60, 70

7. 51, 53, _____, 57, 59

Ordinal Numbers

1. Color the floors.

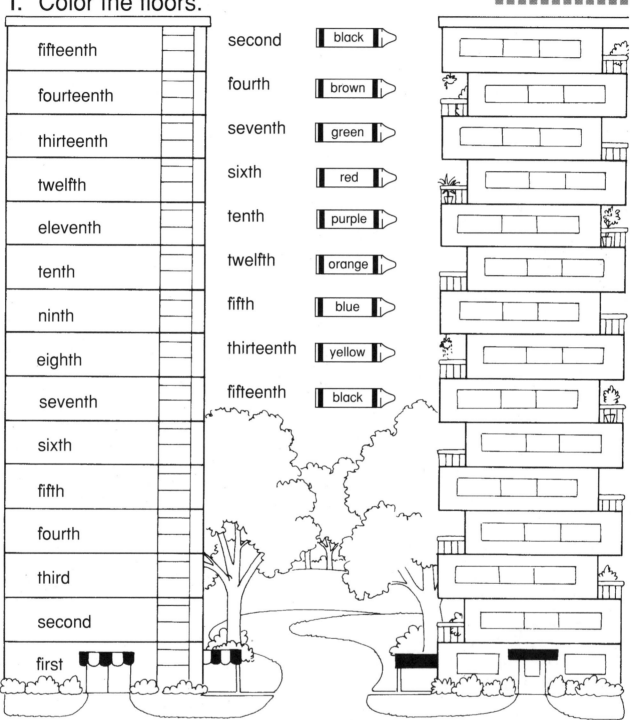

fifteenth	
fourteenth	
thirteenth	
twelfth	
eleventh	
tenth	
ninth	
eighth	
seventh	
sixth	
fifth	
fourth	
third	
second	
first	

second — black

fourth — brown

seventh — green

sixth — red

tenth — purple

twelfth — orange

fifth — blue

thirteenth — yellow

fifteenth — black

Number Sense

Ring the word for the higher floor.

2. ninth   fourth

3. fifteenth   twelfth

Use with text pages 93–94.

Number Patterns

Complete the table.
Write the missing numbers.

1	2	3	4	5	6	7	8	9	10
11			14	15	16	17	18	19	20
21			24	25	26	27	28	29	30
31			34	35	36	37	38	39	40
41			44	45	46	47	48	49	50
51			54	55	56	57	58	59	60
61			64	65	66	67	68	69	70
71			74	75	76	77	78	79	80
81			84	85	86	87	88	89	90
91			94	95	96	97	98	99	100

1. Count by threes to 30. Ring the numbers | purple ▷.
2. Count by twos to 30. Ring the numbers | green ▷.

Reasoning

3. Continue the pattern.

   1, 11, 21, 31, 41, _____, _____

Problem Solving
Extend and Create Patterns

Look for a pattern.
Write the missing numbers.

1. 85, 75, 65, _____, _____, 35, _____, _____, 5

2. 1, 5, 9, 13, _____, _____, _____, _____, 33

3. 49, 47, 45, 43, 41, _____, _____, 35, _____, _____

4. 2, 5, 8, 11, _____, _____, _____, _____, _____

5. 24, 34, 44, _____, _____, _____, _____, _____

Story Corner
Tell a friend about the patterns.

6.

7.

Even and Odd Numbers

Use cubes. Then color to show each number.
Ring even numbers in red.
Ring odd numbers in blue.

If no cubes are left over, the number is even. If I cube is left over, the number is odd.

1. 4 ⟨red⟩

2. 7

3. 1

4. 8

5. 5

6. 2

7. Use cubes.
Ring the even numbers in red.
Ring the odd numbers in blue.

3   7   32   25   6   48   13   41   22

Problem Solving

Add any two even numbers to solve.
Ring the answer.

8. Even Number + Even Number = ?   Even Number

Odd Number

Comparing Numbers

Write each number. Then
ring the greater number.

1.

⑮   12
___   ___

2.

___   ___

Write each number. Ring the
number that is less.

3.

___   ___

4.

___   ___

5.

___   ___

6.

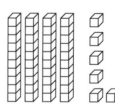

___   ___

Problem Solving

Write the number.

7. I am 3 greater than 72.
I am 1 less than 76.

___

8. I am 5 greater than 61.
I am 3 less than 69.

___

Use with text pages 103–104.

Greater Than and Less Than

Use place-value models to show each pair of numbers.
Then write < or > in each circle.

1. 56 (>) 54   36 ( ) 37   35 ( ) 52

2. 57 ( ) 45   24 ( ) 21   48 ( ) 60

3. 12 ( ) 14   8 ( ) 11   7 ( ) 4

4. 22 ( ) 12   41 ( ) 61   40 ( ) 30

Write your own number sentences.

5. _____ > 64   _____ < 33   17 < _____

6. 29 ( ) _____   _____ ( ) 48   30 ( ) _____

Reasoning

7. Write a number that comes before 75.

    _____

8. Write a number that comes after 75.

    _____

9. Which of the two numbers is greater?

    Write it. _____

Problem-Solving Strategy

Make a Table

Complete the table to find a pattern.

1. Tyrone has a coin collection.
He puts 5 coins in each box.
How many coins
are in 4 boxes?   _____ coins

	1	2	3	
	5	10		

2. Each coin costs 4¢.
Tyrone spent 24¢.
How many coins
did he buy?   _____ coins

	1	2	3			
	4	8	12			

Reasoning

3. How many coins can
Tyrone put in 6 boxes?   _____ coins

Counting Patterns

You need a .

Use your calculator. Finish the counting patterns. Write each number you see.

1. Press

ON/C · 1 · + · 1 · = · = · = · = · =

2 3 ___ ___ ___ ___

2. Press

ON/C · 5 · + · 5 · = · = · = · = · =

___ ___ ___ ___ ___

3. Press

ON/C · 2 · 5 · + · 5 · = · = · = · =

___ ___ ___ ___

Reasoning

4. How can you get your calculator to count by threes?

_____

Counting Pennies, Nickels, and Dimes

Count on to find the total amount.

1.

_5_ ¢ _10_ ¢ _15_ ¢ _16_ ¢ | 16 | ¢

2.

____ ¢ ____ ¢ ____ ¢ ____ ¢ | | ¢

3.

____ ¢ ____ ¢ ____ ¢ ____ ¢ ____ ¢ | | ¢

4.

____ ¢ ____ ¢ ____ ¢ ____ ¢ ____ ¢ ____ ¢ | | ¢

Number Sense

Use punch-out coins.
Trace and write the value on each coin.

5. Use 3 coins to show 15¢.   **6.** Use 4 coins to show 40¢.

HBJ material copyrighted under notice appearing earlier in this work.

Use with text pages 121–122.

Quarter

Count on from 25¢.
Write the total amount.

1.

   $\underline{25}$ ¢ $\underline{35}$ ¢ $\underline{40}$ ¢ $\underline{41}$ ¢ $\boxed{41}$ ¢

2.

   ____ ¢ ____ ¢ ____ ¢ ____ ¢ ____ ¢ $\boxed{}$ ¢

3.

   ____ ¢ ____ ¢ ____ ¢ ____ ¢ ____ ¢ $\boxed{}$ ¢

4.

   ____ ¢ ____ ¢ ____ ¢ ____ ¢ ____ ¢ ____ ¢ $\boxed{}$ ¢

Problem Solving

Use punch-out coins. Solve.

5. Phil has 1 quarter, 2
    nickels, and 1 penny.
    How much money does
    Phil have?
    _____ ¢

6. Anna has 2 nickels. Sam
    has 3 pennies. How
    much more money does
    Anna have?
    _____ ¢ more

Name _____

4.4
■■■■■■■■
■ USE WHAT YOU
■ KNOW
■■■■■■■■

Comparing Money
Greatest Amount

Count on to find the total amounts.
Ring the greatest amount.

1.

_31_ ¢   _25_ ¢   (36) ¢

2.

_____ ¢   _____ ¢   _____ ¢

3.

_____ ¢   _____ ¢   _____ ¢

Reasoning

4. Len has 24¢.
   Tina has 44¢.
   Who can buy the toy?

   _____

33¢

Use with text pages 125–126.

Half Dollar

Which children can buy the book?
Write the amounts.
Then ring the names.

1. (Nancy)

_____50_____ ¢

2. Edith

_____45_____ ¢

3. Glen

_____ ¢

4. Alan

_____ ¢

5. Rita

_____ ¢

6. David

_____ ¢

Visual Thinking

7. Look carefully at a nickel.
   Put it away.
   Picture it in your mind.
   Describe it to a friend.
   Have your friend guess the coin.

It is bigger than a penny. It is....

Problem-Solving Strategy
Make a Model

Use punch-out coins and Workmat 4.
Write the amounts.

1. Robert has I quarter, I dime, and 2 pennies. He spends I dime. How much money does he have now?

    <u>27</u> ¢

2. Nema has 5 nickels and 3 pennies. She spends 3 nickels. How much money does she have now?

    _____ ¢

3. Julia has 2 dimes, 2 nickels, and 2 pennies. She spends I dime and I nickel. How much money does she have left?

    _____ ¢

4. Greg has I quarter, I nickel, and 5 pennies. He finds 5 pennies. How much money does he have?

    _____ ¢

5. Harry has 6 nickels and I penny. He gives 3 nickels to a friend. How much money does he have now?

    _____ ¢

6. Mae has I quarter and 4 nickels. She finds I dime. How much money does Mae have?

    _____ ¢

Story Corner

7. Look at the pictures. Make up a money story. Share it with a friend.

Use with text pages 129–130.

Counting On from 50¢

Count on. Write the total amount.

1.

50 ¢   75 ¢   80 ¢   85 ¢ $\boxed{85}$ ¢

2.

___ ¢   ___ ¢   ___ ¢   ___ ¢ $\boxed{}$ ¢

3.

___ ¢   ___ ¢   ___ ¢   ___ ¢ $\boxed{}$ ¢

4.

___ ¢   ___ ¢   ___ ¢   ___ ¢   ___ ¢ $\boxed{}$ ¢

Visual Thinking

5. Tran has 58¢ in all.
   What coins are left in her bank?
   Write how many.
   Ring the coin name.

_____   dimes   nickels   pennies

Name _____

Combinations of Coins

Count on to find out how much money.
Write the total amount.

_72_ ¢

_____ ¢

3.

_____ ¢

4.

_____ ¢

5.

_____ ¢

6.

_____ ¢

Reasoning

7. John has 67¢.
Ring the belt that he can buy.

Use with text pages 135–136.

Name _____

4.9

■■■■■■■
: **USE WHAT YOU**
: **KNOW**
■■■■■■■■■■

Equal Amounts

Work with a friend.
Use your punch-out coins.
Write the amount.
Work together to find fewer coins to
make the same amount. Draw.
Write the value on each coin.

1.

_55_ ¢

2.

_____ ¢

3.

_____ ¢

Number Sense

4. Which amount could you make with
   the fewest coins? Use punch-out
   coins. Ring the amount.   41¢   51¢   61¢

Counting Change

Work with a friend.
Count up from the price to find the change.
Use punch-out coins to count out the
change to your friend.

1. You have 70¢.
   You buy

   59¢ 60 ¢ 70 ¢

   You have 12 ¢ change.

2. You have 45¢.
   You buy

   39¢ _____ ¢ _____ ¢

   You have _____ ¢ change.

3. You have 65¢.
   You buy

   53 ¢ _____ ¢ _____ ¢ _____ ¢

   You have _____ ¢ change.

Number Sense

Solve. Use punch-out coins.
Trace and write the value on each coin.

4. Janine has 50¢ to spend.
   She buys a pin for 24¢.
   Use the fewest coins possible to show Janine's change.

Problem Solving

Make a Decision

Do you have enough money?
Write the amount. Then ring **Yes** or **No**.

1. You have   . _95_ ¢

Do you have enough money to buy a ? (Yes) No

2. You have   . ____ ¢

Do you have enough money to buy a ?Yes No

3. You have   . ____ ¢

Do you have enough money to buy a ? Yes No

4. You have   . ____ ¢

Do you have enough money to buy a ? Yes No

Number Sense

5. Ring the better estimate.

more than 50¢

less than 50¢

Hour

Draw the hour hand so that both clocks show the same time.

1.

5:00

8:00

2:00

Draw the minute hand so that both clocks show the same time.

2.

10:00

3:00

6:00

Draw the hour hand and the minute hand.

3.

12:00

9:00

1:00

Reasoning

Ring the reasonable answer.

4. Maria eats dinner at _____ .   3:00   6:00

Understanding Time

Hour

Read the time.
Use a punch-out clock.
Show 1 hour later. Then draw hands on
the clock to show 1 hour later.

1.

$4{:}00$

2.

$9{:}00$

3.

$1{:}00$

4.

$10{:}00$

5.

$5{:}00$

6.

$11{:}00$

Problem Solving

Solve. Write the answer.

7. The bus leaves in 1 hour.
It is 2:00 now. What time will the bus leave? ____:____

Name ____

30 Minutes
Half Hour

Write the times.

1.

9:30

2.

3.

Problem Solving

Solve. Write the answer.

4. The bus comes at 8:00. It takes 30 minutes to get to school. What time will the bus get there? __:__

56 P   Use with text pages 155–156.

15 Minutes
Quarter Hour

Write the times.

1.

┌─────────────┐   ┌─────────────┐   ┌─────────────┐
│   5:15   │   │   :   │   │   :   │
└─────────────┘   └─────────────┘   └─────────────┘

2.

┌─────────────┐   ┌─────────────┐   ┌─────────────┐
│   :   │   │   :   │   │   :   │
└─────────────┘   └─────────────┘   └─────────────┘

3.

┌─────────────┐   ┌─────────────┐   ┌─────────────┐
│   :   │   │   :   │   │   :   │
└─────────────┘   └─────────────┘   └─────────────┘

Problem Solving

Use a punch-out clock. Write the times.

4. It is 8:30.
   What time will it be
   in 15 minutes?   _____ :

5. It is 2:15.
   What time will it be
   in 15 minutes?   _____ :

Problem Solving

Use Data

9:00–9:30	9:30–10:30	10:30–12:30	12:30–1:00	1:00–1:30	1:30–2:00	2:00–3:00
Breakfast	Music	Hiking	Lunch	Crafts	Sailing	Swimming

This is Paul's schedule for one day at camp. Read the schedule. Write the answers.

1. When does hiking begin?

   10:30

2. When does hiking end?

   ___:___

3. How long is hiking?

   _____ hours

4. How many minutes pass from the beginning of breakfast until the beginning of music?

   _____ minutes

5. How long is sailing?

   _____ minutes

6. How long is music?

   _____ hour

Number Sense

Ring the better estimate.

7. Paul swims from 2:00 to 3:15.

   He swims for about _____.   a half hour   an hour

Minutes

Write the times.

I.

8:15   ⬛:⬛   ⬛:⬛   ⬛:⬛

2.

⬛:⬛   ⬛:⬛   ⬛:⬛   ⬛:⬛

3.

⬛:⬛   ⬛:⬛   ⬛:⬛   ⬛:⬛

Number Sense

Ring the better answer.

4. Dee jogs until 4:20.
   It is almost _____.

   4:00   4:30

5. Angie swims until 4:55.
   It is almost _____.

   4:30   5:00

Estimating Time

About how long will it take?
Ring the better estimate.

1.

I minute

I hour

to wash hands

2.

I minute

I hour

to play a game

3.

I minute

I hour

to tie a shoe

4.

I minute

I hour

to fix dinner

Story Corner

Ring the correct word to complete each sentence.

5. I take a few ____ to brush my teeth.   minutes   hours

6. I spend two or three ____ at the movies. minutes   hours

Using the Calendar

1992 Calendar

January

S	M	T	W	T	F	S
			1	2	3	4
5	6	7	8	9	10	11
12	13	14	15	16	17	18
19	20	21	22	23	24	25
26	27	28	29	30	31	

February

S	M	T	W	T	F	S
						1
2	3	4	5	6	7	8
9	10	11	12	13	14	15
16	17	18	19	20	21	22
23	24	25	26	37	28	29

March

S	M	T	W	T	F	S
1	2	3	4	5	6	7
8	9	10	11	12	13	14
15	16	17	18	19	20	21
22	23	24	25	26	27	28
29	30	31				

April

S	M	T	W	T	F	S
			1	2	3	4
5	6	7	8	9	10	11
12	13	14	15	16	17	18
19	20	21	22	23	24	25
26	27	28	29	30		

May

S	M	T	W	T	F	S
					1	2
3	4	5	6	7	8	9
10	11	12	13	14	15	16
17	18	19	20	21	22	23
24/31	25	26	27	28	29	30

June

S	M	T	W	T	F	S
	1	2	3	4	5	6
7	8	9	10	11	12	13
14	15	16	17	18	19	20
21	22	23	24	25	26	27
28	29	30				

July

S	M	T	W	T	F	S
			1	2	3	4
5	6	7	8	9	10	11
12	13	14	15	16	17	18
19	20	21	22	23	24	25
26	27	28	29	30	31	

August

S	M	T	W	T	F	S
						1
2	3	4	5	6	7	8
9	10	11	12	13	14	15
16	17	18	19	20	21	22
23/30	24/31	25	26	27	28	29

September

S	M	T	W	T	F	S
		1	2	3	4	5
6	7	8	9	10	11	12
13	14	15	16	17	18	19
20	21	22	23	24	25	26
27	28	29	30			

October

S	M	T	W	T	F	S
				1	2	3
4	5	6	7	8	9	10
11	12	13	14	15	16	17
18	19	20	21	22	23	24
25	26	27	28	29	30	31

November

S	M	T	W	T	F	S
1	2	3	4	5	6	7
8	9	10	11	12	13	14
15	16	17	18	19	20	21
22	23	24	25	26	27	28
29	30					

December

S	M	T	W	T	F	S
		1	2	3	4	5
6	7	8	9	10	11	12
13	14	15	16	17	18	19
20	21	22	23	24	25	26
27	28	29	30	31		

Ring these special dates on the calendar.

1. the first day of June
2. the last day of September
3. Thanksgiving Day, November 26
4. Independence Day, July 4
5. Valentine's Day, February 14
6. Mother's Day, May 10
7. Father's Day, June 21
8. April Fools' Day, April 1

Reasoning

9. Paula's birthday is 7 days before Peter's birthday. Paula's birthday is on Friday. On what day is Peter's birthday?

_____

Name _____

Problem-Solving Strategy

Draw a Picture

The magic hen will lay 1 egg every 5 minutes.
Draw the eggs that will be in the nest
at each time.

1. 10:05   10:10   10:15   10:20

2. 10:25   10:30   10:35   10:40

3. 10:45   10:50   10:55   11:00

Visual Thinking

4. Ring the ice cubes that have been
   in the glass for 30 minutes.

62 P

Use with text pages 169–170.

Understanding Regrouping

Work with a friend.
Use punch-out tens and ones and
Workmat 3. Put in ones to show the top number.
Have your friend put in ones to show
the bottom number. Join the ones.
Complete the table.

	Ones	Join. Write how many.	Can you make a ten? Ring Yes or No.	Trade. Write how many.
1.	8 7	_15_ ones	(Yes) No	_1_ ten _5_ ones
2.	4 5	___ ones	Yes No	___ ten ___ ones
3.	9 4	___ ones	Yes No	___ ten ___ ones
4.	6 6	___ ones	Yes No	___ ten ___ ones

Number Sense

5. Ring the two that name the same number.

I ten 3 ones   I I ones   I3 ones   I ten 0 ones

More Regrouping

You need punch-out tens and ones
and Workmat 3.
Put in tens and ones to show each problem.

Complete the table.

	Show	Join the ones. Write how many.	Can you make a ten? Ring Yes or No.	Trade. Write how many.
1.	13 + 8	11 ones	(Yes) No	2 tens 1 ones
2.	35 + 7	___ ones	Yes No	___ tens ___ ones
3.	68 + 1	___ ones	Yes No	___ tens ___ ones
4.	29 + 9	___ ones	Yes No	___ tens ___ ones
5.	46 + 7	___ ones	Yes No	___ tens ___ ones

Visual Thinking

6. Write how many.

_____ cubes

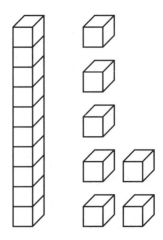

_____ cubes

Understanding 2-Digit Addition

Use punch-out tens and ones
and Workmat 3. Add. Trade if you need to.

1.

tens	ones
2	5
+	8
3	3

tens	ones
4	3
+	7

tens	ones
2	1
+	2

tens	ones
2	8
+	2

2.

tens	ones
2	9
+	2

tens	ones
5	6
+	6

tens	ones
2	3
+	8

tens	ones
6	5
+	9

3.

tens	ones
4	5
+	8

tens	ones
3	3
+	9

tens	ones
5	7
+	5

tens	ones
3	0
+	4

Number Sense

Ring the better estimate.

4. $50 + 30 = 80$, so $42 + 28$ is   greater than 80.
less than 80.

5. $50 + 30 = 80$, so $50 + 35$ is   greater than 80.
less than 80.

Adding 2-Digit Numbers

Use punch-out tens and ones and Workmat 3.
Add. Trade if you need to.

1.

tens	ones
4	2
+ 1	9
6	1

tens	ones
2	9
+ 1	7

tens	ones
4	7
+ 2	9

tens	ones
5	8
+ 1	6

2.

tens	ones
2	7
+ 1	2

tens	ones
1	9
+ 3	2

tens	ones
	5
+ 4	8

tens	ones
2	2
+ 3	8

Problem Solving

Use punch-out tens and ones and Workmat 3.
Solve.

3. Cal had 29 cubes. His
uncle gave him 15 cubes
for his birthday.
Then how many cubes
did Cal have?

4. Wendy had 4 tens and
2 ones. Then she got
3 more tens and 9 more
ones. She traded ones
for a ten. Then how
many tens and ones did
she have?

_____ cubes

_____ tens and _____ ones

More Adding 2-Digit Numbers

Use punch-out tens and ones and Workmat 3.
Find the sum.

1.
$$38 + 38 = 76$$ $$55 + 21$$ $$23 + 45$$ $$29 + 44$$ $$24 + 47$$ $$19 + 28$$

2.
$$84 + 15$$ $$82 + 14$$ $$12 + 28$$ $$37 + 25$$ $$78 + 19$$ $$54 + 27$$

3.
$$68 + 8$$ $$67 + 13$$ $$19 + 3$$ $$26 + 19$$ $$73 + 10$$ $$86 + 7$$

Problem Solving

Ring the answer.

4. Theo had 5 tens and 15 ones. He traded
   10 ones for a ten. Shari had 5 tens and
   12 ones. She traded 10 ones for a ten. After
   that, who had more ones, Theo or Shari?

   Theo   Shari

Name _____

6.6
■■■■■■■■■■■6.6
USE WHAT YOU
KNOW
■■■■■■■■■■■

Addition Practice

Use punch-out tens and ones and Workmat 3.
Add.

1.
$$\begin{array}{r} 19 \\ +28 \\ \hline 47 \end{array}$$
$$\begin{array}{r} 57 \\ +26 \\ \hline \end{array}$$
$$\begin{array}{r} 78 \\ + 7 \\ \hline \end{array}$$
$$\begin{array}{r} 62 \\ +17 \\ \hline \end{array}$$
$$\begin{array}{r} 47 \\ +16 \\ \hline \end{array}$$
$$\begin{array}{r} 28 \\ +37 \\ \hline \end{array}$$

2.
$$\begin{array}{r} 29 \\ +23 \\ \hline \end{array}$$
$$\begin{array}{r} 17 \\ +27 \\ \hline \end{array}$$
$$\begin{array}{r} 6 \\ +76 \\ \hline \end{array}$$
$$\begin{array}{r} 68 \\ + 8 \\ \hline \end{array}$$
$$\begin{array}{r} 24 \\ +27 \\ \hline \end{array}$$
$$\begin{array}{r} 55 \\ + 4 \\ \hline \end{array}$$

3.
$$\begin{array}{r} 37 \\ +25 \\ \hline \end{array}$$
$$\begin{array}{r} 58 \\ + 4 \\ \hline \end{array}$$
$$\begin{array}{r} 19 \\ +36 \\ \hline \end{array}$$
$$\begin{array}{r} 36 \\ +35 \\ \hline \end{array}$$
$$\begin{array}{r} 18 \\ +66 \\ \hline \end{array}$$
$$\begin{array}{r} 36 \\ +57 \\ \hline \end{array}$$

Problem Solving

Solve.

m a t h e m a _ _ _

4. Arturo made a word with his letters.
He got 16 points for the word. He
already had 39 points. What was his
total score?

_____
+ _____
_____

_____ points

_____

Use with text pages 191–192.

Problem Solving

Use Data

Some children voted for their favorite
things to do in the summer. Count the tally marks.
Write the totals in the table.

Summer Activities		
	Tally Marks	Total
	HHT HHT HHT HHT HHT I	26
	HHT HHT HHT II	
	HHT III	
	HHT HHT III	

Answer the questions about the table.

1. How many children like
   to go camping in the
   summer?

   _____ children

2. What is the total number
   who like to skate and
   play baseball?

   _____ children

3. Which summer activity
   did the greatest number
   of children vote for?

   _____

   _____

Story Corner

4. Make up a question
   about the table. Give it
   to a friend to answer.

Finding Reasonable Sums

Ring the best estimate.

1. Kenny has 39 cards.
Kate has 24 cards.
About how many
cards do they have?

about 40   (about 60)   about 80

---

2. Beth has 43 cards.
Jack has 37 cards.
About how many
cards do they have?

about 80   about 30   about 50

---

3. Terry has 52 cards.
Elena has 19 cards.
About how many
cards do they have?

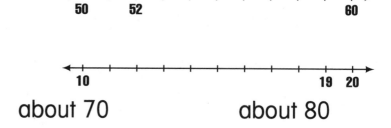

about 60   about 70   about 80

Number Sense
Ring the best estimate.

4. 75 + 16

more than 70   more than 80   more than 90

Use with text pages 195–196.

Adding Money

⟨ Puzzle Sale ⟩

39¢   54¢   44¢   65¢

Use the picture.
Solve. Show your work.

1. Kim bought a
   clown puzzle
   and a boat
   puzzle. How
   much did
   she spend?

   $$\begin{array}{r} 1 \\ 54¢ \\ +39¢ \\ \hline 93¢ \end{array}$$

   93 ¢

2. Ms. Tuma
   bought a boat
   puzzle and a
   tree puzzle.
   How much did
   she spend?

   – _____ ¢
   _____ ¢
   _____ ¢

   _____ ¢

Ring the answer.

3. Carlos spent more than
   60¢ on one puzzle.
   Which puzzle did he buy?   boat   tree   clown   jet

Number Sense

Ring Yes or No.

4. Mark has 95¢. He wants   Yes   No
   to buy a jet puzzle and a
   boat puzzle. Does he
   have enough money?

Problem Solving

Too Little Information

Do you have enough information? If you do, solve.
If you do not, ring the sentence you need.
Then solve. Show your work.

1. In his first turn, Hank moved
   12 spaces on the game board.
   On his next turn, he moved
   11 spaces. How many spaces
   did he move?

   The board has 64 spaces.
   Hank has played the game
   8 times.

   _____ spaces

2. The game has two kinds of
   cards. It has 25 yellow cards.
   How many cards does the
   game have altogether?

   The game has 35 red cards.
   Hank played the game for
   20 minutes.

   _____ cards

Reasoning

Ring the answer.

3. A spinner has 4 numbers. The pattern
   of the numbers is + 2. What do you
   need to know to find the numbers?

   the sum of   any one of the   the first number
   the numbers   numbers

Use with text pages 199–200.

Exploring 2-Digit Subtraction

Use punch-out tens and ones and
Workmat 3. Complete the table.

	Show.	Take away.	Do you need to trade? Ring Yes or No.	Trade if you need to. Write how many are left.
1.	3 tens 4 ones	5 ones	(Yes) No	_2_ tens _9_ ones
2.	4 tens 2 ones	7 ones	Yes No	__ tens __ ones
3.	2 tens 2 ones	9 ones	Yes No	__ tens __ ones
4.	3 tens 7 ones	6 ones	Yes No	__ tens __ ones
5.	5 tens 1 one	8 ones	Yes No	__ tens __ ones
6.	1 ten 9 ones	9 ones	Yes No	__ tens __ ones

Number Sense

7. Ring the better estimate.

$45 - 5 = 40$, so $45 - 8$ is   greater than 40

less than 40

Understanding 2-Digit Subtraction

Use punch-out tens and ones and
Workmat 3. Subtract. Trade if you need to.

1.

tens	ones
3	14
4̸	4̸
−	8
3	6

tens	ones
3	9
−	8

tens	ones
3	1
−	9

tens	ones
4	6
−	5

2.

tens	ones
3	3
−	4

tens	ones
2	4
−	7

tens	ones
2	5
−	8

tens	ones
4	8
−	9

3.

tens	ones
3	2
−	8

tens	ones
7	4
−	7

tens	ones
6	3
−	4

tens	ones
5	5
−	6

Problem Solving

4. There are 59 windows.
   The man has washed 9.
   How many windows
   are left?

   _____ windows _____

5. There are 23 houses.
   The woman has taken
   mail to 8. How many
   houses are left?

   _____ houses _____

2-Digit Subtraction

Do you need to trade? Ring Yes or No.
Subtract. Use punch-out tens and ones
and Workmat 3.

1.

tens	ones	
5	8	Yes
−	3	(No)
5	5	

tens	ones	
4	3	Yes
−	2	No

tens	ones	
3	2	Yes
−	9	No

2.

tens	ones	
3	8	Yes
−	9	No

tens	ones	
3	5	Yes
−	7	No

tens	ones	
8	4	Yes
−	9	No

3.

tens	ones	
4	6	Yes
−	7	No

tens	ones	
3	2	Yes
−	9	No

tens	ones	
9	7	Yes
−	6	No

Number Sense

4. Tamara had 4 dimes and 7 pennies.
She traded one of her dimes for 10
pennies. Write how many dimes
and pennies she has now. _____dimes _____pennies

Name _____

More 2-Digit Subtraction

Do you need to trade?
Ring Yes or No.
Then subtract.

1.
```
  5 15
   6̶5̶    Yes      29  Yes      92  Yes      44  Yes
  -39    No      -17  No      -23  No      -21  No
   26
```

2.
```
   54  Yes      74  Yes      99  Yes      81  Yes
  - 6  No      -57  No      -27  No      -24  No
```

3.
```
   66  Yes      95  Yes      87  Yes      85  Yes
  -29  No      -16  No      - 6  No      -13  No
```

Problem Solving

Solve. Show your work.

4. Glen had 84¢. He paid 25¢ to cross the bridge. How much did he have left?

_____

_____ ¢

5. Nicole had 5 dimes and 7 pennies. She used 25¢ to cross the bridge. What coins did she have left?

_____

____dimes ____pennies

Use with text pages 217–218.

More Subtraction

Subtract. Use the code to find
a secret message. Write the code
letter in the circle under each answer.

1.
$$65 - 39 = 26$$
Ⓘ

29 −17	92 −23	44 −21
◯	◯	◯

54 −6	66 −40	56 −19	94 −15	60 −48
◯	◯	◯	◯	◯

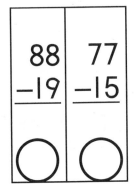

88 −19	77 −15
◯	◯

91 −29	59 −28	97 −25
◯	◯	◯

79 −27	42 −5	85 −48
◯	◯	◯

CODE BOX

12	23	26	31	37	48	52	62	69	72	79
S	W	I	H	O	L	Z	T	A	E	N

Number Sense

2. Use the code. Make up a secret word.
   Write a subtraction sentence for each letter.
   Have a friend find your word.

Problem-Solving Strategy

Make and Use a Graph

A group of children collected jars.
Then they each made a graph.
They colored one jar on the graph
for each jar collected.
Here is Ken's graph.

Jars Collected

Week 1   🫙🫙🫙🫙🫙🫙🫙🫙🫙🫙

Week 2   🫙🫙🫙🫙🫙🫙🫙🫙🫙🫙

Week 3   🫙🫙🫙🫙🫙🫙🫙🫙🫙🫙

Week 4   🫙🫙🫙🫙🫙🫙🫙🫙🫙🫙

Color the jars.
1. Color 9 jars for Week 1.
2. Color 10 jars for Week 2.
3. Color 8 jars for Week 3.
4. Color 5 jars for Week 4.

Find the sum or difference.
5. How many jars did Ken collect
   in all for Weeks 2 and 3?

_____ jars

6. How many more jars did Ken
   collect in Week 1 than in Week 4?

_____ more jars

Visual Thinking

Do these without counting.
7. In which week did Ken
   collect the fewest jars?

Week ___

8. In which week did Ken
   collect the most jars?

Week ___

Checking Subtraction

Subtract. Then check by adding.

1.
$$67 \quad 55$$
$$-12 \quad +12$$
$$55 \quad 67$$

$$87$$
$$-48$$

$$92$$
$$-57$$

2.
$$83$$
$$-77$$

$$45$$
$$-30$$

$$54$$
$$-21$$

3.
$$61$$
$$-32$$

$$80$$
$$-28$$

$$72$$
$$-55$$

Problem Solving

Solve. Show your work.

4. Suki drew 30 pictures last year. Bobby drew 19 pictures last year. How many more pictures did Suki draw?

_____ more pictures

5. Vince drew 27 pictures last year. He drew 15 pictures this year. How many pictures did he draw altogether?

_____ pictures

Adding and Subtracting Money

Add or subtract to solve.

1. Yolanda has 75¢. She buys one goldfish for 67¢. How much money does she have left?

$$\begin{array}{r} {}^{6}\!\!\!\!\;{}^{15}\\ \cancel{75}¢ \\ -67¢ \\ \hline 8¢ \end{array}$$

 _____ ¢

2. Rita buys orange juice for 49¢ and grape juice for 67¢. How much more does the grape juice cost than the orange juice?

_____ ¢

3. Joel buys a pin for 32¢ and a ball for 56¢. How much money does he spend?

_____ ¢

4. Rob has 40¢. He wants to buy a boat that costs 88¢. How much more money does he need?

_____ ¢

Story Corner

Work with a friend.

5. Make up three word problems about buying things. Have your friend write a number sentence for each of your word problems.

1. _____ ◯ _____ = _____

2. _____ ◯ _____ = _____

3. _____ ◯ _____ = _____

Use with text pages 227–228.

Problem Solving

Choose the Operation

Add or subtract to solve.

1. Albert counted 52 movie tapes. The store owner rented 36 of them. How many movie tapes were left?

_____16___ movie tapes

2. Luisa counted 67 music tapes. Her friend Renée counted 14 more. How many music tapes did they count in all?

_____

_____ music tapes

3. Jeff has 37 tapes. Keith has 13 tapes. How many more tapes does Jeff have than Keith?

_____

_____ more tapes

Reasoning

Ring the best estimate.

4. Georgia used 11 tapes to fill a box. About how many tapes would she use to fill 4 boxes?

about 30
about 40
about 50

Addition and Subtraction Practice

Add or subtract. Find a pattern.
Connect the dots for the two sets of
answers, from least to greatest.

Make a picture
of a tugboat.

$$\begin{array}{r} 54 \\ +33 \\ \hline 87 \end{array}$$

$$\begin{array}{r} 54 \\ -42 \\ \hline 12 \end{array}$$

Start

Start

$$\begin{array}{r} 54 \\ +34 \end{array}$$

$$\begin{array}{r} 54 \\ -41 \end{array}$$

$$\begin{array}{r} 54 \\ -40 \end{array}$$

$$\begin{array}{r} 54 \\ +36 \end{array}$$

$$\begin{array}{r} 54 \\ +35 \end{array}$$

$$\begin{array}{r} 54 \\ -39 \end{array}$$

$$\begin{array}{r} 54 \\ -38 \end{array}$$

$$\begin{array}{r} 54 \\ +39 \end{array}$$

$$\begin{array}{r} 54 \\ +38 \end{array}$$

$$\begin{array}{r} 54 \\ +37 \end{array}$$

$$\begin{array}{r} 54 \\ -37 \end{array}$$

$$\begin{array}{r} 54 \\ +40 \end{array}$$

$$\begin{array}{r} 54 \\ +41 \end{array}$$

$$\begin{array}{r} 54 \\ +42 \end{array}$$

$$\begin{array}{r} 54 \\ -33 \end{array}$$

$$\begin{array}{r} 54 \\ -34 \end{array}$$

$$\begin{array}{r} 54 \\ -35 \end{array}$$

$$\begin{array}{r} 54 \\ -36 \end{array}$$

Story Corner

Make up a word problem about
cars and trucks in a city. Have a
friend solve your problem.

Use with text pages 231–232.

Problem-Solving Strategy

Use Data

CESAR'S SPORTING GOODS

87 BASEBALLS	92 FOOTBALLS	36 SOCCER BALLS
79 BASKETBALLS	56 VOLLEYBALLS	43 GOLF BALLS

Use the poster to solve the problems.

1. How many more footballs are there than volleyballs?

$$92$$
$$-56$$
$$\overline{36}$$

_36_ more footballs

2. How many golf balls and soccer balls are there?

_____ _____ balls

3. How many volleyballs and golf balls are there?

_____ _____ balls

4. How many more basketballs are there than soccer balls?

_____ _____ more basketballs

5. 58 baseballs were sold. How many were not sold?

_____ _____ baseballs

6. 47 basketballs were sold. How many were not sold?

_____ _____ basketballs

Identifying Solid Shapes

1. Color each shape.

 green

 orange

 red

 yellow

 purple

 blue

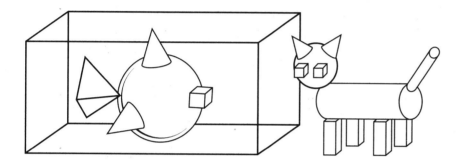

2. Count each shape.
Write how many.

3

____

____ △

____ (cylinder)

____ ○

____ △ (pyramid)

Visual Thinking

3. Tell a friend about one of the
shapes on this page.
Have your friend guess the shape.

Making Solid Shapes

Use cubes. Make the shape.
Tell how many cubes you used.

1.

_____ cubes

2.

_____ cubes

Visual Thinking

3. Ring the shapes that have a round
   bottom or a round top.

   cone   cube   cylinder

4. Ring the shapes that have corners.

   cube   rectangular prism   sphere

Making Plane Figures

1. Color inside the circles blue.
   Color inside the triangles orange.
   Color inside the rectangles red.

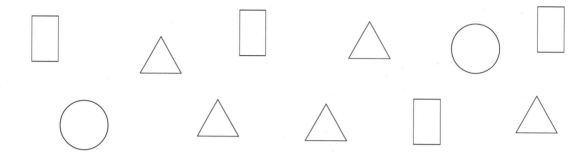

2. Count each shape. Write how many.

   __2__ circles   _____ triangles   _____ rectangles

3. Color inside the triangles purple.
   Color inside the circles red.
   Color inside the squares green.

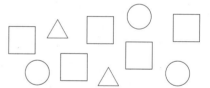

4. How many are there? Count each shape.
   Write how many.

   _____ triangles   _____ circles   _____ squares

Visual Thinking

5. If you traced around the widest part
   of a cone, what plane figure would you draw?

   rectangle   circle   triangle

Sides and Corners

1. Draw a shape that has 8 sides and 8 corners.

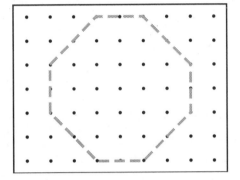

2. Draw a shape that has 5 sides and 5 corners.

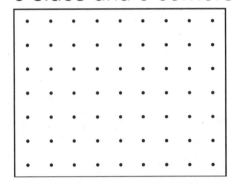

3. Draw a shape that has 3 sides and 3 corners.

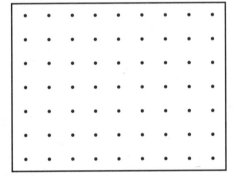

4. Draw a shape that has 4 sides and 4 corners. All 4 sides are the same length.

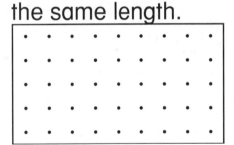

Visual Thinking

5. In this box, draw a shape that has sides and corners. Cover it.

   Describe it to a friend. Have your friend draw it. Compare your shape with the one your friend drew.

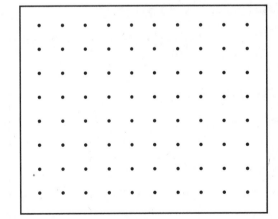

8.5
USE WHAT YOU KNOW

Extending a Pattern

Draw the shape that continues the pattern.

1.
_____

2.
_____

3.
_____

4.
_____

5.
_____

6.
_____

Visual Thinking

Draw the shape that continues the pattern.

7.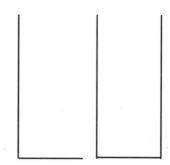
_____

Use with text pages 251–252.

Congruent Figures

Look at each figure.
Use a geoboard to make a figure that is
the same size and shape.
Draw your figure.

1.

2.

3.

4.

5.

6.

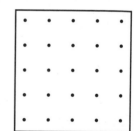

Reasoning

7. Use a pattern block. Copy this design.

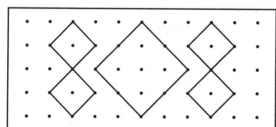

Problem-Solving Strategy

Make a Table

1. Some children made this funny bird.
   How many of each shape did they use?
   Complete the table to find out.

Our Funny Bird

Shape	Number
◯	2
▢	
▭	
△	

2. How many rectangles would there be in
   4 funny birds like this one?
   Make a table to find out.

birds	1	2	3	4
rectangles	5	___	___	___

Problem Solving

Use the table to answer the questions.

3. How many rectangles
   would there be in 4
   funny birds?

   _____

4. How many rectangles
   would there be in 3
   funny birds?

   _____

Symmetry

Draw one line of symmetry for each shape.

1.

2.

Draw two lines of symmetry for each shape.

3.

  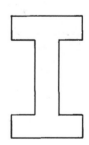

Visual Thinking

4. Ring the shape if it could be folded to make a line of symmetry.

Equal Parts

Write the number of equal parts.

1.

8

_____   _____   _____   _____

2.

_____   _____   _____   _____

3.

   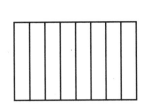

_____   _____   _____   _____

4.

   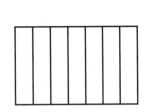

_____   _____   _____   _____

Problem Solving

5. Four friends want to share two cookies in equal parts. Show how they can divide them.

Fractions

1. Color $\frac{1}{3}$.

---

2. Color $\frac{1}{4}$.

---

3. Color $\frac{1}{8}$.

Reasoning

Ring **Yes** or **No**.

4. Henry colored $\frac{1}{2}$ of a circle.

Marsha colored $\frac{1}{2}$ of a larger circle.

Did they color the same amount?

　　　　Yes　　　　　　　　No

More Fractions

Complete each fraction to show
what part is shaded.

1. $\dfrac{1}{2}$ $\dfrac{}{3}$ $\dfrac{}{4}$

2. $\dfrac{}{8}$ $\dfrac{}{6}$ $\dfrac{}{5}$

Write a fraction to show what part is shaded.

3. $\dfrac{2}{8}$ $\dfrac{}{}$ $\dfrac{}{}$

4. $\dfrac{}{}$ $\dfrac{}{}$ 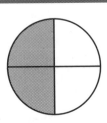 $\dfrac{}{}$

Visual Thinking

5. Ring the fractions that
are the same size.

  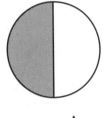

    $\dfrac{1}{2}$ $\dfrac{1}{3}$ $\dfrac{2}{4}$

Use with text pages 265–266.

Parts of Groups

Color to show the fractions.

1.

$\frac{1}{3}$ green, $\frac{2}{3}$ yellow

2.

$\frac{2}{3}$ orange, $\frac{1}{3}$ red

3.

$\frac{2}{5}$ blue, $\frac{3}{5}$ orange

4.

$\frac{4}{5}$ purple, $\frac{1}{5}$ yellow

5.

$\frac{3}{4}$ green, $\frac{1}{4}$ purple

6.

$\frac{4}{6}$ red, $\frac{2}{6}$ blue

Problem Solving

Color. Write the answer.

7. There are 4 trees.

$\frac{1}{4}$ of the trees are yellow.

The rest are orange.

How many trees are orange?

_____ trees

Probability

Use a pencil and a paper clip
to make a spinner. Predict
which color the spinner
will stop on more often.
Ring the color.

black   gray

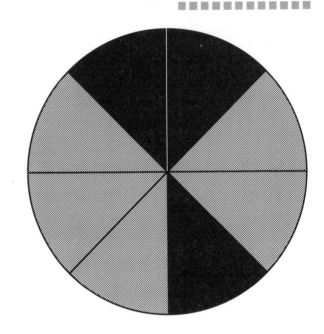

Spin the paper clip 10 times. Color the chart to
show where the spinner stops after each spin.

Spin	1	2	3	4	5	6	7	8	9	10
Black										
Gray										

Reasoning

Color the spinner so that it
will stop on black more often
than on gray. Try your
spinner.

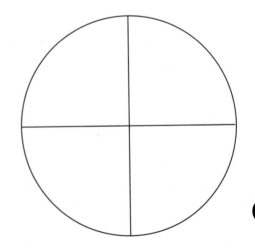

Use with text pages 269–270.

Name _____

Problem-Solving Strategy

Draw a Picture

Some friends shared a cake.
Each decorated part of the cake.

Sara put raisins on her part.

Linda put nuts on her part.

Olga put coconut on her part.

Franco put lemon rings on his part.

Jack put blueberries on his part.

Kale put strawberries on his part.

1. Draw the cake so that each person gets an equal part.

Visual Thinking

Draw a picture to solve.
Ring the answer.

2. Sam and Elena shared a
chicken pie. Sam ate $\frac{1}{4}$ of
the pie. Elena ate $\frac{2}{4}$.
How much pie
was left?

$\frac{1}{4}$ $\frac{2}{4}$ $\frac{3}{4}$

Use with text pages 271–272.

Measuring Length

Use cubes to
measure each brush.
Write the length.

1.

about ___4___ cubes

2.

about _____ cubes

3.

about _____ cubes

4.

about _____ cubes

Visual Thinking

5. Ring the longer box.

Use with text pages 281–282.

Name _____

Inches and Feet

Use an inch ruler to draw pieces of yarn.

1. 2 inches

2. 5 inches

3. 3 inches

Ring in green the longest piece of yarn.
Ring in red the shortest piece of yarn.

Number Sense

Think about the real object.
Ring the better estimate.

4.

longer than 1 foot   longer than 1 foot

shorter than 1 foot   shorter than 1 foot

Name _____

9.3
■■■■■■■■
USE WHAT YOU
KNOW
■■■■■■■■

Problem-Solving Strategy
Estimate and Measure

Ring the reasonable answer.
Then use an inch ruler to measure the
length to the nearest inch.
Write the length.

		Estimate	Measure
1.	an eraser	I inch (7 inches) 20 inches	about _____ inches
2.	your thumb	2 inches 9 inches I5 inches	about _____ inches
3.	a calculator	25 inches I5 inches 5 inches	about _____ inches

Number Sense

Write an estimate.

4.   about _____ long

Use with text pages 285–286.

Estimating and Measuring Weight

Nonstandard Units

Ring the one that weighs more.

1.

2.

3.

4.

5.

6.

Ring the objects that weigh less than you weigh.

7.

Story Corner

8. Work with a friend. Tell some things that weigh more than you weigh.

Estimating and Measuring Weight

Pounds

About how much does each weigh?
Ring the answer.

I.

about I pound
(more than I pound)
less than I pound

2.

about I pound
more than I pound
less than I pound

3.

about one pound
more than I pound
less than I pound

4.

about one pound
more than I pound
less than I pound

Reasoning

Ring the correct picture.

5.

6.

Use with text pages 289–290.

Quarts, Pints, and Cups

Which hold the same amounts?
Color the cups to show the amount.

1.
Pint

2.
Quart

Solve.

3. Darren has 1 pint of juice. How many cups can he fill?

_____2_____ cups

4. Marta has 1 quart of juice. How many cups can she fill?

_____ cups

---

5. Lani has 3 cups of juice. Beth has 1 quart of juice. Who has more juice?

_____

- -

_____

6. Kim has 1 quart of juice. He drinks 1 cup of it. How much does he have left?

_____

- -

_____

Number Sense

Ring the better estimate.

7.

more than 1 quart
less than 1 quart

8.

more than 1 cup
less than 1 cup

Choose the Appropriate Tool

Ring the right tool for the job.

1. To find the length of a board

2. To find the amount of juice in a bottle

3. To find out whether a rock weighs more than a shell

4. To find the length of a nail

Story Corner

5. Work with a friend. Pretend you are making a bird feeder. Tell what tools you would use to measure.

Use with text pages 293–294.

Centimeters

Use your centimeter ruler to draw pieces of yarn.

1. 7 centimeters

2. 3 centimeters

3. 11 centimeters

This string is 10 centimeters long. It is 1 decimeter long. Work with a friend.

4. Measure and cut a string that is as long as a decimeter. Use your string to find something in the classroom that is longer. Write the name of the object you found. _____

Number Sense

5. Hal's card is 3 centimeters wider than Meg's. Meg's card is 7 centimeters wide. How wide is Hal's card?

_____ centimeters

Perimeter

Use your centimeter ruler to measure the perimeter.

I.

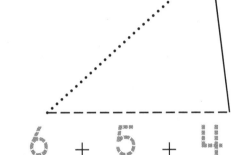

$\underline{6} + \underline{5} + \underline{4} = \underline{15}$ centimeters

The perimeter of the triangle is $\underline{15}$ centimeters.

2.

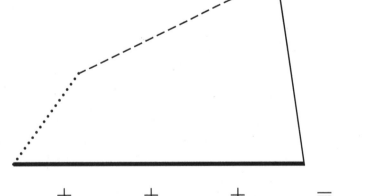

____ + ____ + ____ + ____ = ____ centimeters

3.

____ + ____ + ____ + ____ = ____ centimeters

Kilograms

Read each scale. Then write the weight.

1.

_____ kilogram

_____ kilograms

_____ kilograms

2.

_____ kilograms

_____ kilogram

_____ kilograms

Reasoning

Ring the better estimate.

3. About how much does a brick weigh?

2 kilograms   20 kilograms

4. About how much does a book weigh?

1 kilogram   10 kilograms

Volume

Use cubes and a box.
Solve. Then ring the answer.

1. Emilio made a shape that was 2 cubes wide and 2 cubes high and 3 cubes deep. How many cubes did he use?

   10   (12)   14

2. Angie made a shape with 24 cubes. George made a shape with 32 cubes. Who made the smaller shape?

   Angie   George

3. Winona filled a box with cubes. She covered the bottom of the box with 20 cubes. Three layers of cubes filled the box. How many cubes were in the box?

   40   50   60

4. Greg covered the bottom of a box with 12 cubes. He needed 2 more layers to fill the box. How many more cubes did he need?

   24   36   48

Visual Thinking

5. Ring the cubes that are easier to count.

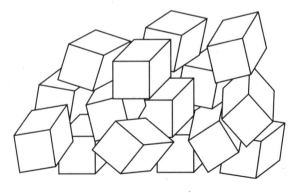

Temperature

Fahrenheit and Celsius

Use a Fahrenheit thermometer and a red crayon.

1. Look at the thermometer. Color to show the temperature.

2. Put the thermometer in a glass of hot water. Wait 5 minutes. Read the temperature. Color to show the temperature.

Use a Celsius thermometer and a red crayon.

3. Look at the thermometer. Color to show the temperature.

4. Put the thermometer on an ice cube. Wait 5 minutes. Read the temperature. Color to show the temperature.

Number Sense

Ring the better estimate.

5. 30 degrees Fahrenheit
   90 degrees Fahrenheit

Problem-Solving Strategy

Guess and Check

How many 1-inch punch-out squares will
fit in each space?
First, write your guess.
Then use 1-inch squares to check.

1.

Guess. _____ squares   Check. __10__ squares

2.

Guess. _____ squares   Check. _____ squares

3.

Guess. _____ squares

Check. _____ squares

Use with text pages 307–308.

Exploring Hundreds

Use hundreds to show each number.
Write the number.

1.   2 hundred 200

2.   4 hundred ____

3.   6 hundred ____

4.   8 hundred ____

5.   9 hundred ____

6.   7 hundred ____

7.   5 hundred ____

8.   3 hundred ____

9.   1 hundred ____

Number Sense

Write the numbers.

10.   ____

11.   ____

Exploring 3-Digit Numbers

Count. Write the number.

1.

___3___ hundreds   ___2___ tens   ___4___ ones   __324__

2.

_____ hundreds   _____ tens   _____ one   _____

3.

_____ hundreds   _____ tens   _____ ones   _____

Reasoning

Ring the most reasonable answer.

4. Cliff is _____ years older than his brother.

8   80   800

5. There are _____ children in the full school bus.

4   40   400

6. There are _____ seats in the movie house.

2   20   200

7. The movie is _____ hours long.

3   30   300

Use with text pages 321–322.

Name _____

Understanding Hundreds, Tens, and Ones

Work with a friend.
Use place-value models and Workmat 5.

1. Show the number. Add 10 more. Continue adding 10 more. Complete the table.

	hundreds	tens	ones
640	6	4	0
650	6	5	0

2. Show the number. Add 100 more. Continue adding 100 more. Complete the table.

	hundreds	tens	ones
300	3	0	0

Number Sense

Ring the models that show the same number.
Use place-value models if you need to.

3.

Writing Numbers to 999

Look at the models.
Write how many in the chart.
Then write the number.

1.

hundreds	tens	ones
5	4	3

543

2.

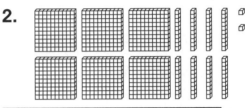

hundreds	tens	ones

_____

3.

hundreds	tens	ones

_____

4.

hundreds	tens	ones

_____

5.

hundreds	tens	ones

_____

6.

hundreds	tens	ones

_____

Number Sense

7. Write the number that is
10 greater than 173.

_____

8. Write the number that is
100 greater than 731.

_____

Place Value

Read the number in the chart. Write how many.

1.

hundreds	tens	ones
7	2	8

__7__ hundreds   _700_

__2__ tens   _20_

__8__ ones   _8_

hundreds	tens	ones
2	7	8

____ hundreds   ____

____ tens   ____

____ ones   ____

2.

hundreds	tens	ones
5	1	6

____ hundreds

____ tens

____ ones

hundreds	tens	ones
6	5	1

____ hundreds   ____

____ tens   ____

____ ones   ____

3.

hundreds	tens	ones
4	3	7

____ hundreds   ____

____ tens   ____

____ ones   ____

hundreds	tens	ones
3	4	7

____ hundreds   ____

____ tens   ____

____ ones   ____

Number Sense

4. Lucas has 7 ones and 9 hundreds. What number is he showing? ____

5. Vicki has 2 tens and 6 hundreds. What number is she showing? ____

More Place Value

Write the number.

1. 4 hundreds 8 tens 7 ones   487
   ____

2. 500 + 50 + 2
   ____

3. 800 + 7
   ____

4. 6 hundreds 1 ten 1 one
   ____

Work with a friend.

5. Fill in the puzzle.

Across

1. 199 + 1
2. 400 + 50
4. 3, 6, _____, 12
5. 7 hundreds 1 ten 8 ones
6. 400 + 50 + 6
9. 700 + 80 + 9
11. 5 hundreds 7 tens 3 ones
13. 200 + 300
14. 4, 8, 12, _____
15. 1 more than 997

Down

1. 2 hundreds 9 tens 4 ones
2. 4 hundreds 1 ten 7 ones
3. 500 + 80 + 8
7. 500 + 50 + 5
8. 6 hundreds 7 tens
10. 900 + 6
12. 1 more than 308
14. 9, _____, 27, 36

Number Sense

6. Write the number that is 3 hundreds less than 640. _____

Problem-Solving Strategy

Make a Bar Graph

What is the favorite forest animal of your classmates?
Ask each child in your class to choose
his or her favorite animal.
Write a tally mark ╱ to show each answer.
Find the total for each animal. Then
complete your graph.

1.

Animal	Tally Marks	Total
Rabbit		
Squirrel		
Deer		
Raccoon		

2.

Favorite Animal

Rabbit															
Squirrel															
Deer															
Raccoon															

0 1 2 3 4 5 6 7 8 9 10 11 12 13 14 15

Visual Thinking

3. Which bar on your graph shows
you the least favorite animal?
Ring it.   longest bar   shortest bar

After, Before, Between

Count.
Write the number that comes after.

1. 333, 334   549, _____   385, _____

2. 241, _____   709, _____   400, _____

Count.
Write the number that comes before.

3. _____, 694   _____, 377   _____, 249

4. _____, 599   _____, 320   _____, 201

Count.
Write the number that comes between.

5. 562, _____, 564   375, _____, 377   872, _____, 874

6. 363, _____, 365   542, _____, 544   299, _____, 301

Visual Thinking

Draw the missing shapes.

7. heart, diamond, heart, diamond, heart, _____, _____,
   diamond, heart

8. diamond, diamond, heart, diamond, diamond, heart,
   _____, _____, heart, diamond, diamond

Comparing Numbers

Write each number.
Compare. Then ring the number that is less.

1.

3 1 4
_____

_____

2.

_____

_____

3.

_____

_____

4.

_____

_____

Number Sense

Use place-value models to compare.
Then ring the number that is less.

5.

167	578	823	424	169
176	478	923	323	109

More Comparing Numbers

Write < or > in the ◯ .

1. 139 ◯ 193   390 ◯ 391   421 ◯ 422

2. 598 ◯ 498   401 ◯ 441   509 ◯ 501

3. 777 ◯ 771   902 ◯ 992   120 ◯ 102

4. 99 ◯ 100   999 ◯ 99   287 ◯ 267

5. 302 ◯ 320   675 ◯ 576   110 ◯ 101

Number Sense

Write the numbers in order from least to greatest.
Use place-value models if you need to.

6. 13, 621, 27, 98, 109, 56, 129

13, _____, _____, _____, _____, _____, 621

82, 208, 802, 28, 280, 820

28, _____, _____, _____, _____, _____

Use with text pages 339–340.

Counting Patterns

Use your calculator. Write each number
you see.

1. Press

$\boxed{\text{ON/C}}$ $\boxed{2}$ $\boxed{0}$ $\boxed{+}$ $\boxed{=}$ $\boxed{=}$ $\boxed{=}$ $\boxed{=}$ $\boxed{=}$

20 40 ___ ___ ___

2. Press

$\boxed{\text{ON/C}}$ $\boxed{5}$ $\boxed{7}$ $\boxed{+}$ $\boxed{1}$ $\boxed{0}$ $\boxed{=}$ $\boxed{=}$ $\boxed{=}$

___ ___ ___

3. Press

$\boxed{\text{ON/C}}$ $\boxed{9}$ $\boxed{+}$ $\boxed{1}$ $\boxed{0}$ $\boxed{0}$ $\boxed{=}$ $\boxed{=}$ $\boxed{=}$

___ ___ ___

Reasoning
Write each number.

4. I am 50 less than 300.
   I am 10 more than 240.
   What number am I?

   ___

5. I am 100 more than 830.
   I am 50 less than 980.
   What number am I?

   ___

Dollar

Work with a friend.
Use punch-out coins and Workmat 4.
Take turns showing ways to make $1.00.
Write how many.

1.	1	1	0	0	25
2.					
3.					
4.					
5.					

Number Sense

6. Ring the coins that show the same
amount of money.

Dollar and Cents

Ring how much money is needed.
Use punch-out money to help you.

1.

2.

3.

4.

Problem Solving

5. Nick has 1 dollar and 3 nickels. Lola has 5 quarters. Write how much each child has. Then ring the greater amount.

    Nick has _____

    Lola has _____

6. Debra has .
   She wants to buy [$1.30].
   Does she have enough money?
   Ring **Yes** or **No**.

    Yes

    No

Problem Solving

Write Appropriate Questions

This table shows how many books the
second-grade classes collected for a
book sale.

Number of Books Collected

Room Number	Reading	Science	Math	Social Studies	Geography
130	19	17	11	7	4
131	18	15	18	13	5
132	9	10	13	8	14

Look at the table. Ring the questions
that you can answer by using the table.

1. How many books did Room 133 collect?

   How many science books were collected?

2. Which room collected the most math books?

   How many music books did Room 132 collect?

3. Write a question that you can answer by using this table.

   _____

   -

   _____

   -

   _____

Story Corner

4. Make up other questions about this
   table. Tell them to a friend.
   Have your friend answer each question.

Adding Hundreds

Look for a pattern.
Add in your head. Then write the sums.

1.
$$\begin{array}{r} 2 \\ +2 \\ \hline 4 \end{array} \qquad \begin{array}{r} 2 \\ +3 \\ \hline \end{array} \qquad \begin{array}{r} 2 \\ +4 \\ \hline \end{array} \qquad \begin{array}{r} 2 \\ +5 \\ \hline \end{array} \qquad \begin{array}{r} 2 \\ +6 \\ \hline \end{array} \qquad \begin{array}{r} 2 \\ +7 \\ \hline \end{array}$$

2.
$$\begin{array}{r} 20 \\ +20 \\ \hline \end{array} \qquad \begin{array}{r} 20 \\ +30 \\ \hline \end{array} \qquad \begin{array}{r} 20 \\ +40 \\ \hline \end{array} \qquad \begin{array}{r} 20 \\ +50 \\ \hline \end{array} \qquad \begin{array}{r} 20 \\ +60 \\ \hline \end{array} \qquad \begin{array}{r} 20 \\ +70 \\ \hline \end{array}$$

3.
$$\begin{array}{r} 200 \\ +200 \\ \hline \end{array} \qquad \begin{array}{r} 200 \\ +300 \\ \hline \end{array} \qquad \begin{array}{r} 200 \\ +400 \\ \hline \end{array} \qquad \begin{array}{r} 200 \\ +500 \\ \hline \end{array} \qquad \begin{array}{r} 200 \\ +600 \\ \hline \end{array} \qquad \begin{array}{r} 200 \\ +700 \\ \hline \end{array}$$

4.
$$\begin{array}{r} 100 \\ +800 \\ \hline \end{array} \qquad \begin{array}{r} 100 \\ +700 \\ \hline \end{array} \qquad \begin{array}{r} 100 \\ +600 \\ \hline \end{array} \qquad \begin{array}{r} 100 \\ +500 \\ \hline \end{array} \qquad \begin{array}{r} 100 \\ +400 \\ \hline \end{array} \qquad \begin{array}{r} 100 \\ +300 \\ \hline \end{array}$$

Visual Thinking

5. Match each problem to the model that shows the sum.

$$\begin{array}{r} 9 \\ +5 \\ \hline \end{array}$$

$$\begin{array}{r} 90 \\ +50 \\ \hline \end{array}$$

Exploring 3-Digit Addition

Use place-value models and Workmat 5.
Find the sums. Trade if you need to.

1.

hundreds	tens	ones
	1	
3	6	8
+ 1	1	3
4	8	1

hundreds	tens	ones
	☐	
1	8	7
+ 2	1	2

hundreds	tens	ones
	☐	
7	3	4
+	3	6

2.

hundreds	tens	ones
	☐	
4	1	3
+ 3	1	9

hundreds	tens	ones
	☐	
5	5	5
+	4	3

hundreds	tens	ones
	☐	
6	2	7
+ 2	4	6

Number Sense

Ring your estimate.

Remember
< means less than
> means greater than

3.   400
       + 300

The sum is < 500.

The sum is > 500.

4.   100
       + 700

The sum is < 900.

The sum is > 900.

Name _____

Understanding 3-Digit Addition

Use place-value models and Workmat 5. Add.

1.

hundreds	tens	ones
2	3	7
+ 5	0	2
7	3	9

hundreds	tens	ones
4	2	9
+ 1	1	6

hundreds	tens	ones
3	3	8
+ 2	2	6

2.

hundreds	tens	ones
2	2	5
+ 1	6	6

hundreds	tens	ones
3	6	8
+ 1	1	1

hundreds	tens	ones
2	0	3
+ 2	5	8

3.

hundreds	tens	ones
7	3	9
+ 1	4	2

hundreds	tens	ones
3	6	7
+	1	3

hundreds	tens	ones
5	2	3
+ 1	0	6

Problem Solving

Solve.

4. There are 329 cans of peanuts. There are 221 cans of walnuts. How many cans of nuts are there in all?

_____ cans

5. Rick counted 102 boxes of oat cereal. He counted 89 boxes of corn cereal. How many boxes of cereal did he count in all?

_____ boxes

Adding 3-Digit Numbers

Use place-value models and Workmat 5. Add.

1.

hundreds	tens	ones
2	7	3
+ 1	6	4
4	3	7

hundreds	tens	ones
5	6	1
+	1	9

hundreds	tens	ones
2	7	8
+ 2	1	1

2.

hundreds	tens	ones
3	5	4
+ 3	0	6

hundreds	tens	ones
6	7	0
+ 2	4	9

hundreds	tens	ones
4	0	5
+ 5	2	8

3.

834	242	468	106	333	691
+ 82	+ 666	+ 426	+ 516	+ 465	+ 118

Problem Solving

Solve. Use a calculator.

4. Ian clipped the wool of 348 sheep. Nell clipped 292 sheep. How many sheep did they clip in all?

_____ sheep.

5. There are 168 hours in one week. How many hours are in 2 weeks?

_____ hours

More Adding 3-Digit Numbers

Add.

1.
$$\begin{array}{r} 629 \\ +154 \\ \hline 783 \end{array}$$
$$\begin{array}{r} 439 \\ +258 \\ \hline \end{array}$$
$$\begin{array}{r} 432 \\ +483 \\ \hline \end{array}$$
$$\begin{array}{r} 562 \\ +396 \\ \hline \end{array}$$
$$\begin{array}{r} 135 \\ +593 \\ \hline \end{array}$$

2.
$$\begin{array}{r} 537 \\ +23 \\ \hline \end{array}$$
$$\begin{array}{r} 516 \\ +133 \\ \hline \end{array}$$
$$\begin{array}{r} 608 \\ +347 \\ \hline \end{array}$$
$$\begin{array}{r} 320 \\ +497 \\ \hline \end{array}$$
$$\begin{array}{r} 256 \\ +316 \\ \hline \end{array}$$

3.
$$\begin{array}{r} 725 \\ +154 \\ \hline \end{array}$$
$$\begin{array}{r} 154 \\ +29 \\ \hline \end{array}$$
$$\begin{array}{r} 390 \\ +595 \\ \hline \end{array}$$
$$\begin{array}{r} 456 \\ +293 \\ \hline \end{array}$$
$$\begin{array}{r} 708 \\ +58 \\ \hline \end{array}$$

Problem Solving

Solve.

4. The supermarket has 134 cans of vegetables and 290 cans of fruit. How many cans are there in all?

_____ cans

5. There are 236 bottles of apple juice and 328 bottles of grape juice. How many bottles are there in all?

_____ bottles

Problem Solving

Use a Graph

Follow these directions.
Draw a ring at the crossing point.

1. Start at 0. Go → 3. Go ↑ 6.
   Draw an orange ring at the crossing point.

2. Start at 0. Go → 1. Go ↑ 3.
   Draw a black ring at the crossing point.

3. Start at 0. Go → 5. Go ↑ 5.
   Draw a red ring at the crossing point.

4. Start at 0. Go → 7. Go ↑ 4.
   Draw a green ring at the crossing point.

Reasoning

5. Start at 0. Go → 6. Go ← 6.
   Where are you? Ring the answer.

   0   3   6

Subtracting Hundreds

Look for a pattern.
Subtract in your head. Then write the difference.

1.

7	7	7	7	7	7
$-\ 6$	$-\ 5$	$-\ 4$	$-\ 3$	$-\ 2$	$-\ 1$

2.

70	70	70	70	70	70
$-\ 60$	$-\ 50$	$-\ 40$	$-\ 30$	$-\ 20$	$-\ 10$

3.

700	700	700	700	700	700
$-\ 600$	$-\ 500$	$-\ 400$	$-\ 300$	$-\ 200$	$-\ 100$

Solve. Use a , ⟋ .

4. $400 + 400 - 300 - 100 =$ _____

5. $300 - 200 + 600 + 200 =$ _____

Visual Thinking

6. Match each problem to the model that shows the
    difference.

$$\begin{array}{r} 12 \\ -\ 8 \\ \hline \end{array}$$

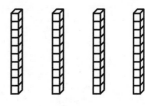

$$\begin{array}{r} 120 \\ -\ 80 \\ \hline \end{array}$$

Exploring 3-Digit Subtraction

Use place-value models and Workmat 5.
Find the difference. Trade if you need to.

1.

hundreds	tens	ones
	7	*11*
2	8̸	1̸
− 1	6	4
1	*1*	*7*

hundreds	tens	ones
	□	□
6	7	3
− 4	4	9

hundreds	tens	ones
	□	□
8	8	7
− 3	2	8

2.

hundreds	tens	ones
	□	□
4	5	6
− 1	2	8

hundreds	tens	ones
	□	□
4	9	0
− 1	7	2

hundreds	tens	ones
	□	□
6	5	4
− 3	3	8

3.

hundreds	tens	ones
	□	□
4	2	1
− 2	1	6

hundreds	tens	ones
	□	□
3	4	2
−	2	4

hundreds	tens	ones
	□	□
5	8	1
− 1	5	9

Number Sense

Ring the better estimate.

4.   500
      − 100
      _____

The difference < 300.

The difference > 300.

5.   500
      − 300
      _____

The difference < 300.

The difference > 300.

Understanding 3-Digit Subtraction

Use place-value models and Workmat 5.
Find the differences. Trade if you need to.

1.

hundreds	tens	ones
	5	18
7	6̸	8̸
− 3	2	9
4	3	9

hundreds	tens	ones
8	5	3
− 4	0	5

hundreds	tens	ones
6	8	2
−	1	7

2.

hundreds	tens	ones
6	3	5
− 1	0	7

hundreds	tens	ones
7	5	4
− 6	2	5

hundreds	tens	ones
8	2	3
− 5	1	2

3.

$$576 - 69 \qquad 472 - 256 \qquad 683 - 244 \qquad 756 - 135 \qquad 470 - 244$$

Problem Solving

4. There are 352 monkeys and 218 lions in the park. How many more monkeys are there than lions?

5. There are 250 hippos in the park. 32 hippos are babies. The rest are adults. How many adult hippos are there?

_____ more monkeys

_____ adult hippos

Subtracting 3-Digit Numbers

Use place-value models and Workmat 5. Subtract.

1.

hundreds	tens	ones
4	1	9
−2	2	5
1	9	4

hundreds	tens	ones
5	7	6
−1	8	3

hundreds	tens	ones
2	3	5
−	1	8

2.

hundreds	tens	ones
8	2	1
−5	0	1

hundreds	tens	ones
6	4	2
−2	7	1

hundreds	tens	ones
7	3	3
−3	4	3

3.

$$958 - 42 \qquad 600 - 200 \qquad 313 - 182 \qquad 504 - 372 \qquad 972 - 656$$

Problem Solving

Solve.

4. Use your calculator. Subtract. Then read the answer upside down. Write the word.

$$864 - 519 \qquad \text{_____}$$

5. The teacher has 442 math books and 327 science books. How many more math books than science books does he have?

_____ more math books

Use with text pages 377–378.

Estimating Sums and Differences

About how much does each bunch of flowers cost?
Write the amount.

1.

$1.00 _____ _____ _____

First, estimate the total cost.
Then use a calculator to find the total cost.

2.

 $1.19 $3.87 $4.28

 $3.87 $2.67 $1.19

Estimate: $5.00   Estimate: _____   Estimate: _____

Answer: $5.06   Answer: _____   Answer: _____

Number Sense

3. About how much is left? Ring the better estimate.
Use a calculator to find the answer.

$3.00
−$1.19
$2.00
$3.00

$6.00
−$3.87
$2.00
$3.00

$5.00
−$4.28
$2.00
$1.00

Problem Solving
Identify Reasonable Results

Bagel with Cheese	$1.49	2 Pickles	$1.10
1 pound of Potato Salad	$2.85	Hero Sandwich	$4.40
Tuna Fish Sandwich	$3.75		

Estimate to find if the total cost is reasonable.
Then ring **Yes** or **No**.

1. Renée buys a bagel with cheese
   and 2 pickles. The total cost is
   about $1.00.

   $1.00
   +$1.00
   ————
   $2.00

   Yes (No)

2. Pablo buys 1 tuna fish sandwich
   and 1 pound of potato salad.
   The total cost is about $5.00.

   _____

   Yes   No

3. Adrienne buys 1 hero sandwich
   and 2 pickles. The total cost is
   about $5.00.

   _____

   Yes   No

Reasoning

4. Ring the better estimate.
   Evan buys a bagel with cheese.
   He pays $2.00.

   The change is < $1.00.   The change is > $1.00.

Making Equal Groups

Work with a friend.
Use cubes to show equal groups.
Then draw equal groups of dots on the
clown hats.

1. 2 groups of 4

2. 3 groups of 4

3. 3 groups of 2

4. 4 groups of 5

Number Sense

5. Ring the picture that shows equal
groups.

Exploring Multiplication with 2 and 5

Ring groups of 2 shoes. Complete the
sentences to find out how many shoes there are.

1.

$2 + 2 + 2 =$ ___6___

3 equal groups of 2 = ___6___

___3___ x 2 = ___6___

2.

$2 + 2 + 2 + 2 =$ _____

4 equal groups of 2 = _____

_____ x 2 = _____

3.

$2 + 2 =$ _____

2 equal groups of 2 = _____

_____ x 2 = _____

4.

$2 + 2 + 2 + 2 + 2 =$ _____

5 equal groups of 2 = _____

_____ x 2 = _____

Problem Solving

Use cubes and Workmat 6.
Write a number sentence to solve.

5. There were 5 jugglers in
the circus. Each juggler
had 5 balls. How many
balls were there?

_____ x _____ = _____

_____ balls

6. There were 5 circus
wagons. In each wagon
there were 3 circus dogs.
How many dogs were there?

_____ x _____ = _____

_____ dogs

Multiplying with 3 and 4

Use punch-out dollars and Workmat 6.
Complete the multiplication sentences.

1.

Ring groups of 3.

_2_ x $3 = $ _6_

2.

Ring groups of 3.

____ x $3 = $ ____

3.

Ring groups of 4.

____ x $4 = $ ____

4.

Ring groups of 4.

____ x $4 = $ ____

Visual Thinking

Ring the answer.

5. Which stacks would be higher,
   4 stacks of 5 umbrellas, or
   5 stacks of 4 umbrellas?

   4 stacks of 5 umbrellas

   5 stacks of 4 umbrellas

Vertical Multiplication

Use cubes. Write the multiplication fact both ways.

1.

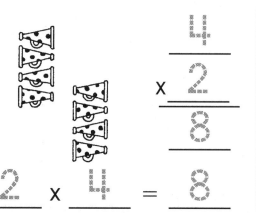

$$\begin{array}{r} 4 \\ \times\ 2 \\ \hline 8 \end{array}$$

___ 2 ___ x ___ 4 ___ = ___ 8 ___

2.

x _____

_____

___ x ___ = ___

3.

x _____

_____

___ x ___ = ___

4.

x _____

_____

___ x ___ = ___

5.

x _____

_____

___ x ___ = ___

6.

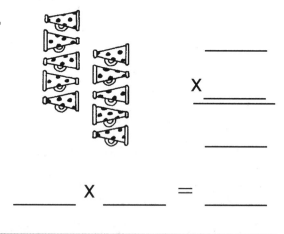

x _____

_____

___ x ___ = ___

Story Corner

7. Make up a clown story about any
multiplication fact. Tell your story
to a friend. Write the fact two ways.

Understanding Multiplication

Use cubes and Workmat 6.
Write each product.

1.

$1 \times 3 =$ ___ 3 ___

2.

$4 \times 1 =$ _____

3.

$4 \times 5 =$ _____

4.

$2 \times 4 =$ _____

Use cubes. Multiply.

5.

$\begin{array}{r} 2 \\ \times 1 \\ \hline \end{array}$
$\qquad$
$\begin{array}{r} 1 \\ \times 5 \\ \hline \end{array}$
$\qquad$
$\begin{array}{r} 4 \\ \times 1 \\ \hline \end{array}$
$\qquad$
$\begin{array}{r} 1 \\ \times 1 \\ \hline \end{array}$
$\qquad$
$\begin{array}{r} 3 \\ \times 1 \\ \hline \end{array}$

Reasoning

Use cubes and Workmat 6. Ring the answer.

6. Put 1 group of 0 cubes on your mat. Put 2 groups of 0 cubes on your mat. How many cubes are on your mat?

7. You have 4 baskets. There are 0 apples in each basket. How many apples do you have in all?

2 cubes   1 cube   0 cubes

0 apples   2 apples   4 apples

Problem Solving

Use a Graph

Children Who Went to the Circus

Group A	👤	👤	👤	👤	👤
Group B	👤	👤	👤	👤	
Group C	👤	👤			
Group D	👤	👤	👤		

Each 👤 stands for 4 children.

Read the table. Then answer each question.

1. How many children in Group D went to the circus?

   __12__ children

2. How many children in Group B went to the circus?

   _____ children

3. Which group has the fewest children who went to the circus?

   Group _____

4. What is the total number of children in Groups A and C who went to the circus?

   _____ children

Reasoning

Suppose each 👤 meant 2 children. Ring the answers.

5. Would your answer to question 3 change?

   Yes   No

6. What would your answer to question 2 be now?

   8 children   32 children

Use with text pages 401–402.

Multiplication in Any Order

Use punch-out hankies.
Write the number sentence.

1.

$$\underline{4} \times \underline{5} = \underline{20}$$

2.

$$\underline{5} \times \underline{4} = \underline{20}$$

3.

$$\underline{} \times \underline{} = \underline{}$$

4.

$$\underline{} \times \underline{} = \underline{}$$

5.

$$\underline{} \times \underline{} = \underline{}$$

6.

$$\underline{} \times \underline{} = \underline{}$$

Story Corner

7. Work with a friend.
   Tell a story about the picture.
   Then write a number sentence.

_____

- - - - - - - - - - - - - - - - - - - -

_____

Multiplying with a Calculator

Use a calculator for skip-counting
and multiplying.

1. Alicia has 4 clown hats.
   Each hat has 3 feathers.
   How many feathers are
   there in all?

   $3 + 3 + 3 + 3 =$ ___**12**___

   $4 \times 3 =$ ___**12**___

2. There are 3 circus rings.
   There are 3 elephants in
   each ring. How many
   elephants are in the rings?

   $3 + 3 + 3 =$ _____

   $3 \times 3 =$ _____

3. There are 5 horses. There
   are 2 riders on each horse.
   How many riders are
   there?

   $2 + 2 + 2 + 2 + 2 =$ _____

   $5 \times 2 =$ _____

4. Tran bought 4 tickets.
   Each ticket cost $5.
   How much did he
   spend?

   $\$5 + \$5 + \$5 + \$5 = \$$ _____

   $4 \times \$5 = \$$ _____

Problem Solving

Write a number sentence. Solve.
Use counters if you need to.

5. The circus was in town
   for 2 weeks. There were
   4 shows each week.
   How many shows were
   there in all?

   _____ X _____ = _____

6. There are 4 circus tents
   with 1 clown in each.
   How many clowns are
   there?

   _____ X _____ = _____

Name _____

12.9
■■■■■■■■■■
■ USE WHAT YOU
■ KNOW
■■■■■■■■■■

Problem Solving

Choose the Operation

Use cubes.
Write a number sentence to solve.

1. A toy clown costs $4. Anna buys 2 clowns. How much money does she spend?

$$\underline{2} \; \bigotimes \; \underline{4} = \underline{8}$$

$$\$ \; \underline{8}$$

2. Owen draws 21 circus pictures. Julie draws 16 pictures. How many more pictures does Owen draw than Julie?

$$\underline{\quad} \bigcirc \underline{\quad} = \underline{\quad}$$

_____ more pictures

3. Nancy ate 8 peanuts. Paul ate 9 peanuts. Lita ate 7 peanuts. Altogether, how many peanuts did they eat?

$$\underline{\ }\bigcirc\underline{\ }\bigcirc\underline{\ } = \underline{\ }$$

_____ peanuts

4. Jay has 5 toy circus tents. He puts 4 toy tigers in each. How many tigers are there?

$$\underline{\quad} \bigcirc \underline{\quad} = \underline{\quad}$$

_____ tigers

Story Corner

5. Tell a friend a story about the picture. Make up a problem. Have your friend write a number sentence to solve it.

$$\underline{\quad} \bigcirc \underline{\quad} = \underline{\quad}$$

Exploring Division: Sharing

Use counters and Workmat 6.
Show how many are in each group.

1.

Ring 2 equal groups.
How many are in each

group? __2__

2.

Ring 3 equal groups.
How many are in each

group? _____

3.

Ring 3 equal groups.
How many are in each

group? _____

4.

Ring 2 equal groups.
How many are in each

group? _____

Reasoning

Can you make 2 equal groups?
Ring **Yes** or **No**.

Yes   No

Yes   No

Yes   No

Exploring Division: Separating

Use counters and Workmat 6.
Show how many groups.

1.

Ring groups of 2.

How many groups? _5_

2.

Ring groups of 4.

How many groups? _____

3.

Ring groups of 3.

How many groups? _____

4.

Ring groups of 5.

How many groups? _____

Reasoning

5. How many clowns can wear

   8 shoes? _____

6. How many shoes are needed

   for 5 clowns? _____

Problem-Solving Strategy

Draw a Picture

Draw a picture to solve.

1. There are 9 fish.
    There are 3 fish in each fishbowl.
    How many fishbowls are there?

    __3__ fishbowls

2. There are 12 pillows.
    There are 4 pillows on each sofa.
    How many sofas are there?

    _____ sofas

3. There are 15 crayons.
    There are 3 crayons in each box.
    How many boxes are there?

    _____ boxes

Reasoning

Ring the answer. Then draw a picture to check.

4. You have 20 stickers. Which would use more pages?

    putting 4 stickers on each page

    putting 5 stickers on each page